40,000 TO ONE

BEN PETRICK

with Scott Brown

Foreword by Clint Hurdle

ISBN-10: 0615583458
ISBN-13: 978-0615583457

DEDICATION

For my three girls, Kellie, Makena and Madison.

Thank you for your sacrifice, love and support.

— *Ben* —

***

For my dad,

who held my hand during the last five minutes

of "Field of Dreams," even though I was 18 at the time.

— *Scott* —

CONTENTS

ACKNOWLEDGMENTS

I want to first thank my parents, siblings and their families for their steadfast support. Without it, I have no idea where my life would be.

I would also like to thank all of our dear friends for their incredible efforts in supporting us through the years, particularly times when I was in the hospital.

To my in-laws, who have been unwavering in their support of me, I can't thank you enough or describe what your understanding has meant.

I want to thank all of the coaches and teachers who taught me a thing or two about dealing with adversity. Those lessons have been useful, to say the least.

To all my doctors and caretakers, particularly those at OHSU, your brilliance and persistence can't be overstated.

Thank you to Steve Wulf of ESPN for bringing my story to a national audience with such nuance and care, and to Jeff Bradley, for bringing my story to Steve.

Finally, I want to thank Scott Brown for his friendship and guidance. Without him, this book wouldn't exist.

— *Ben Petrick*

PRAISE FOR *40,000 TO ONE*

"Ben Petrick could've become the best catcher in baseball, and maybe one of the best in history, until Young-Onset Parkinson's robbed him of his physical abilities. But as *40,000 to One* shows, he lost one gift only to find another."

— **Steve Wulf,** *ESPN The Magazine* —

"Ben's love for his daughter — the 'One' in the title — is awe-inspiring. There are moments in this book that take your breath away. Having known Ben since he was 12, I've had a front-row seat for his dramatic life story. What I've always known, and what the world will know once they've read *40,000 to One*, is his baseball success was prologue to what Ben was really meant to do in life: reveal a better way to those of us whose lives spin wildly at times."

— **Steve Ballmer, CEO, Microsoft** —

"Ben writes with a kind of honesty and grace that both breaks your heart and makes it soar. He makes me want to be not just a better writer, but a better person. Never maudlin and truly inspiring, Ben and his book are a treasure."

— Sharon Randall, nationally syndicated columnist —

"An inspiration for all."

— Tracy Ringolsby, *Baseball America* —

"Looking back, I'm amazed at what Ben accomplished. It's hard enough performing at the highest levels of baseball, which he did. On top of that, he had to fight off a disease that robbed him of his physical ability. And on top of that, he had to play under the tremendous pressure of hiding the effects of that disease. (That said) I'm more impressed by what he's done with his life since he left the game."

— Todd Helton, first baseman, Colorado Rockies —

"Ben's courageous book, *40,000 to One*, is a huge step forward in raising awareness and hope for Parkinson's sufferers. I'm proud to call him a friend."

— Matt Holliday, outfielder, St. Louis Cardinals —

"Ben has made himself uncommon. Life's tried to tear him down, but he continues to give rather than take."

— Clint Hurdle, manager, Pittsburgh Pirates —

"*40,000 to One* is a must-read … Powerful, inspiring and challenging on every level."

— Scott Brosius, 1998 World Series MVP —

"A courageous and brilliantly told book."

— Dan O'Dowd, general manager, Colorado Rockies —

"There are men with talent, and men with gifts. Ben had a talent for baseball, but you'll discover his true gift is something much, much bigger."

— Brian Grant, NBA veteran —

"The book's final story, 'Night Becomes Us,' will have you out of your seat, applauding and wiping tears from your eyes. As a new father, I can't stop thinking about it."

— Adam Melhuse, MLB veteran —

"Ben has a voice that needs to be heard. I can relate to so much of his experience with Parkinson's, as well as his life as a father and a son. He has an exceptional gift for defining the essence of things, both the good and the not-so-good, and his wisdom is priceless."

— Davis Phinney, Olympic medalist and Tour de France stage winner; author of *The Happiness of Pursuit*; founder of the Davis Phinney Foundation —

"The same traits that made Ben excel as an athlete are helping him do the same today as a person, husband and father. These intimate, revealing and touching accounts of his struggle show what champions are made of."

— Dr. John Nutt, Co-founder and Director of the OHSU Parkinson Center of Oregon —

"Ben's stories — particularly 'Night Becomes Us' — speak volumes to me. I thank him for shedding light into my life, and for inspiring me to become a better father."

— Brent Butler, MLB veteran —

"I'm highly confident that Ben's stories will inspire bravery and resilience in all who read them."

— Julie Carter, ANP, Professor of Neurology, Associate Director, OHSU Parkinson Center of Oregon —

ABOUT THIS BOOK

This book has an unorthodox structure that bears some explanation, as it does not take the form of a traditional autobiography.

Over the past year, Ben Petrick has gained notoriety for the personal stories he's written for his website, Faith in the Game. Many of these stories are at the heart of the book, along with a dozen new ones.

These stories are preceded by a prologue, which is meant to provide an overview of Bens' life and context for the stories that follow. You'll also find a foreword by Ben's former manager, Clint Hurdle, who is now the skipper of the Pittsburgh Pirates.

The title of this book, *40,000 to One*, has two meanings. First, Americans have a 1-in-40,000 chance of being stricken with Parkinson's disease. The second meaning, which is more personal, is revealed later in the book …

BEFORE I BEGIN …

Dear Reader,

I'm pretty sure J.K. Rowling doesn't start her books by giving up any pretense of cool, but I can't help myself.

This is probably a rookie mistake, but I want to thank you in advance for the time you're about to spend reading *40,000 to One*.

I'm very proud of this book, but have one concern: It worries me that you might interpret mentions of my statistics and accomplishments in these stories as boastful. Please know I mention these only to illustrate the extremes between life before and after my diagnosis with Parkinson's disease.

Humility is extremely important to me, and trust me, I realize I have a few things working against me, author-wise. For example:

1. You've probably never heard of me.

2. I have a highly unpleasant disease.

3. I think "author-wise" is a word.

I think we can all acknowledge this is not the starting place for a Pulitzer hopeful. So why did I write this book?

Because I'm the son, brother and husband of great people, and I thought I was destined for greatness, too. I felt my life would be one thing, until it became something very different, with a "before" and "after" that were as unalike as lightning and lightning bugs. I had to figure out who I was, now that I was no longer who I used to be.

In other words, I'm all of us. We all get thrown sooner or later. Maybe it's a death, a divorce or a job loss.

We all break.

And when we do, it's easy to turn inward. Our natural inclination is to try to regain what we've lost. This is reinforced by a society that promotes the self; that tells us to make ourselves whole so that we can one day help others again.

I'm here to present you with an opposing idea.

One of the perils of illness is that it makes you feel useless. Lord knows, I felt this way. But as you'll read, the greatest gift I gave myself was the recognition that I was still needed.

Adversity, no matter its form, is such an internal process. But I'm here to tell you that getting outside yourself can save you. The more you focus on those who need you — the more you allow yourself to be needed — the more you'll be helped. My experience is salvation comes not in the love you get, but the love you give.

You've been slammed with a cold fist. You're on your knees. Believe me, I get it.

For more than a decade I felt like life had promised me a piano, but only gave me half the keys. In an instant, the body that had been my greatest asset became my greatest liability. There was no note, no forensics and no explanation. All I knew was that I was confused and exhausted, not to mention terrified this was the *best* I'd ever feel again.

The prophesy of my life had been turned upside down. One day, I was on my way to fame and a multi-million dollar career; the next, I was living in anonymity and receiving disability checks in the mail.

One day I was displaying physical gifts that made people say, "I guess you had to be there," to anyone who wasn't in attendance; the next, I was weighing and measuring each movement with the same trepidation a toddler would.

I'd always envisioned myself fading into immortality. Instead, all I did was fade.

Blessedly, a chain of events you'll read about here made me realize *this* was my moment. Baseball made me feel special, but it was losing the game I loved that allowed me to find out if I was truly uncommon.

Until I retired and became a dad, I'd spent most of my adult life with 25 other guys, either on planes or in an office we called a "clubhouse." But my daughter only wanted her hair put in pigtails and for me to get on the floor and play princess.

I'm not sure how we made it work, but we did. We created our own short hand; a patented set of unspoken inflections between my precocious 2-year-old and her odd father. I bobbed and weaved, and — with a mercy my baby girl inherited from her mother — she waited for me.

In return, I slowly lowered myself to the floor, and I played princess. And it was awesome.

I found that a person barely three feet tall was capable of giving me something 40,000 couldn't: a feeling of being so loved that I wanted to take action and embrace the future.

At one point, it filled me sadness that my kid never got to see me play baseball. Now I feel my on-field accomplishments are a distant second to the achievement of getting out of my chair, commanding my knees to bend and playing princess.

The greater our adversity, the greater our purpose. You may no longer be a person in motion, but you can always be a person of action. Be it in your life or mine, I've come to believe there are no wrong numbers in life.

I guess that's another reason I'm uncomfortable with statistics.

Thank you again for reading *40,000 to One*.

FOREWORD,
BY CLINT HURDLE

This is not a baseball book.

At least, it's not *only* a baseball book.

It's definitely not a pull-the-string story by a could've-been-great athlete who made something of his life only after he survived years of being his own worst enemy. Those stories have become all too common — and Ben Petrick is anything but common.

I first came into contact with Ben in 1995 when he was 18 and I was a roving hitting instructor in the Colorado Rockies organization. The first day of Instructional League, he was doing things in the hitting area that guys on the Major League roster couldn't. He'd spit line drive after line drive into the back of the batting cage; his throws from home to second came so fast they virtually bent the infield grass as they whizzed past; and his time in the 40-yard-dash was the fastest in the entire organization. This would have been remarkable for a center fielder. But as an 18-year-old catcher, he was an athlete from another planet.

Ben was the epitome of a five-tool player — six, if you include his ability to handle pitchers — and full of what you might call "competitive greatness." He could have been one of the greats of his generation, and maybe even redefined the catching position. He had no ceiling.

Most importantly, Ben just had an unshakable decency about him. He stood out without trying to stand out. He always had a laugh ready for his teammates, and he was disgustingly humble. Despite his obvious star power, Ben said all he wanted to do was become a partner in a golf course when he retired so he could "mow grass in the morning, and cut people's hair in the afternoon."

And he was appreciative. Most of us have to lose everything to understand things Ben did when he was just a teenager, which is probably attributable to his remarkable parents. He was one of the few kids you didn't have to tell to stop and watch a sunset.

When I met Ben, I was still putting to rest afflictions that had derailed my career and two marriages. I was just learning how to fill the voids in my life with something other than alcohol and excess; straining to put faith and family before myself.

I'd done a lot of living in my 40 years, and there were very few secrets a young guy could reveal to me that I'd have considered surprising.

But Ben shocked me.

When he was diagnosed with Parkinson's disease, Ben confided in me and asked what I thought could be the greater meaning in such a thing.

I was uncommonly speechless. Just a few months earlier, Ben had been called up by the Rockies and became the toast of Denver. There was no scenario in which this kid wouldn't be a 10-year major leaguer with multiple All Star appearances. His star could not have been higher. What could possibly be the meaning of stealing all of that, and replacing it with a disease this boy already loathed for what it was doing to his father?

As time went on, though, I began to see the common ground between us. I did know what it was like to go from feeling like you have this gravitational pull toward greatness, and then suddenly have a disease take you in the other direction.

I understood the weight of expectation, and the prison talent builds for us from time to time.

This bond made it all the more agonizing to watch a kid who'd never been inclined to break a heart, have his heart broken before my eyes.

Part of being a pro athlete is coming to terms with the fact that the majority of sentiments about you are either totally false or highly flawed. You have to make peace with this if you want to survive.

But when fans booed Ben, he should have blown up. When writers used him as a metaphor for unfulfilled expectations, calling every underperforming prospect "Petrick 2.0," he had every right to scream.

I certainly wanted to scream, but he never did — not once. Ben never used Parkinson's as an excuse. And when he did finally reveal his secret to the world when he retired, the impact of Ben's grace was profound.

I took Ben's actions to heart when I was fired by the Rockies in 2009, less than two years after I was part of a group that helped lead the team to the World Series. As my dismissal was happening, I reminded myself of Ben's example, thinking, "The best statement I can make about who I am and what I believe will be in the way that I accept this adversity. Anyone can be grateful when they arrive, but how many can do it when they exit? Be thankful and feel blessed by the opportunity."

What I wish I'd told Ben when he was diagnosed is that we are all on a journey. I wish I'd said that life will take us on some incredible adventures if we keep our eyes and hearts open.

But I couldn't say those things then, because Ben hadn't taught them to me yet.

As you'll find in this book, Ben's struggles have been real and profound. His search for meaning has taken him to some dark places.

But by living and telling his story, Ben's become a husband, father, coach and man of God who is uncommon in every way. He doesn't do things to get things. He does them because they're the right things to do for others. Having this capacity for good is so much bigger than winning a World Series ring, to the power of a million.

I may have some additional insight in that I'm the parent of a child with health concerns, as my young daughter suffers from a rare condition that presents her with major challenges. My hope is she can live to understand the greater meaning of her suffering, and bestow that wisdom on others. That's what Ben is doing now, and I have to think that his parents have never been prouder of him than they are today.

When I was about 30 and coming off a broken marriage, my father took me for a walk. He said, "Life's not fair, boy. You need to get this. You need to listen to me. You don't need to talk. This isn't the time for your questions. Life's not fair. What you do in situations you're handed is going to dictate how you're going to live your life, how you're going to respect your life, and what you'll make of your life."

Truer words never graced my ears. Life is about how you take on the hard times, however brutal they may be. It's about living your life with such transparency that others can learn from the burden you're carrying. It's about what you do when life's not fair.

Ben's greeted each challenge with exceptional dignity. He's figured out the big secrets in life. He's found "it." Life has shaken him; tried to tear him down. But he's refused to give into anything but his better angels. I've seen a servant's heart jump out of Ben. I've seen light spring from him when everything could have turned dark.

Somewhere along the line, my angels provided me with a student who could teach me something. Every reader of this book is fortunate to have the same opportunity to learn through Ben's example.

Clint Hurdle joined the Colorado Rockies organization as a minor league hitting instructor in 1994; serving in that capacity until he was named the Rockies hitting coach in 1997. He was promoted to manager in the middle of the 2002 season, and served in that capacity until May 2009. In 2007, he managed the club to its first World Series appearance.

Today, Hurdle is entering his second season as Pittsburgh Pirates manager. At the 2011 All-Star Break, the Pirates had a 47-43 record, and were one game out of first place in the NL Central. It was the first time the Pirates had been over .500 going into the All-Star break since winning the 1992 National League East.

Hurdle is national spokesperson for Prader-Willi Syndrome, which afflicts his daughter, Madison. To find out more about the cause, please visit www.pwsausa.org.

MERELY PROLOGUE

There's a line at the beginning of the movie "Gone Baby Gone" that goes: "Funny how it's the things you don't choose that makes you who you are. Your city, your neighborhood, your family. People take pride in those things, like it was something they accomplished."

When I retired from baseball in 2004, I was keenly aware that two things I never chose had nonetheless defined my life. For 22 years, I was unique in my athletic ability; five years later, as the only known professional athlete to have his career ended by Parkinson's disease, I was unique in my disability.

In 1995, I was drafted straight out of high school by the Colorado Rockies. An executive with the club told my father he wouldn't be surprised if I had a 15-year career and ended up in the Hall of Fame someday. When I packed up and left my hometown of Hillsboro, Ore., I was the object of everyone's envy; when I returned, I was the object of everyone's pity. A guy who seemed destined to be remembered forever was now well down the road toward being forgotten.

There was a saying posted in the Rockies weight room that I had adopted as my personal mission statement after I was called up to the big leagues in Sept. 1999:

The vision of a champion is someone who is bent over, drenched in sweat, at the point of exhaustion, when nobody else is watching.

But as the words "I'm retiring because I have Parkinson's disease" left my mouth in 2004, revealing my secret to the world for the first time, I was left to wonder: What had been the point of all those countless hours spent drenched in sweat when no one else was watching? When all was said and done, I was back in Hillsboro, the symbol of a disease that was as much my choosing as the place where I was born.

Of all the disappointments that came to a head that day, none packed a greater punch than my realization that the saying on the weight room wall was fraudulent. I'd played nine professional seasons, and all it had amounted to was a freakish sideshow legacy.

Saul Bellow wrote that "any artist should be grateful for a naïve grace which puts him beyond the need to reason elaborately."

My only wish on the day I retired was that I could go back to being that rookie, all alone and drenched in sweat, and drift in that innocent white space a little bit longer.

Thinking I had a voice.

Thinking I had a say.

Thinking this life was mine.

The seven years after my retirement contained happiness (including marriage and the birth of our first daughter) as well as its counterweight (the daily torment that I might be holding them back from better lives). For me, there was no greater hell than the creeping feeling that I was a curse to my blessings.

Then, at the end of those seven years, came this realization:

You know that kid, all alone and drenched in sweat, thinking he had a say in his life … ?

He was right.

When I retired at 27, I thought my life story had been told. Imagine my surprise when I discovered those years were merely prologue — the end of my beginning.

Only after I stopped playing baseball did the pages start to count.

**

What I thought would be my story — but I now understand to merely be my *backstory* — begins with Hungry-Hungry Hippo Day:

My best friend Erik and I are playing the game in my room, each of us trying to get our hippo to gobble more marbles than the other. My brother, Rian, who is more than four years older than I am, enters loudly, takes over the game, and the taunting begins, same as always. But on this particular day, I lose my composure. On this particular day, I kick Rian — the quarterback, the baseball star, the Petrick Bros. heavyweight champ — in the jaw. For a brief moment, we make eye contact. I dart for the exit and manage to hit the stairs one second before he does.

I blow through our front door and into the daylight, the oaks that cantilever our road rushing past. As I sprint down the lane, I'm conscious of the absence of Rian's fingertips on my shirt, and that the thrum of his feet hitting the ground is growing fainter. I realize — and so does he — that I'm faster.

Blocks away, it occurs to me I must eventually head home, and when I do Rian pounds my arm as though he's trying drive a nail through it. But now we both know that he can't catch me.

Soon I can't get enough of these challenges. Every summer the high school where my father is athletic director holds football camps. A handful of coaches are playing against two-dozen fifth and sixth graders. I'm a third grader watching on the sidelines, when a coach waves me into the game. "Benji is on our team," he says.

Soon I'm catching long bombs and juking tacklers. When the next season rolls around, I'm asked to play on a team with kids three grades above me.

As an eighth grader, I long jump 19 feet, three inches — the equivalent of leaping from the high school three-point line to a spot directly beneath the basketball rim.

My senior year of high school, I'm the Oregon offensive player of the year in football, and we win the state title. I run a 4.5-second 40-yard dash, bench press 305 pounds, and am recruited as a safety to several Pac 10 schools. But there's no question baseball will be my sport, and on the weekends I fly out on recruiting trips to Miami, Arizona and Arizona State. I decide to sign a letter of intent to play for the Sun Devils.

This doesn't deter pro scouts, though, who tell me they think I'll be the next on a short list of great Oregon baseball players that includes Johnny Pesky, Bobby Doerr, Dale Murphy, Danny Ainge and Harold Reynolds.

Coming off basketball, I have one practice before our first baseball game. I take batting practice with 15 scouts lined up around the cage. The next day, around 30 scouts come to our first game. It's been raining, and the scouts help my dad rake and line the field so they'll get a chance to see me play. I go 4-for-4.

Soon after, I go 5-for-6 with five home runs over two games. I hit .700 for most of the season before finishing at .526.

In the local newspaper, my dad is quoted as saying this:

> **"When you're a coach or athletic director, you dream one of your players is going to reach the top, and that he'll be a good, humble young man,**

too. So it feels wonderful when that young man turns out to be your son."

Cameras follow me around school on draft day. We think the Mets might draft me with the 16th pick, but they and others are scared off by the prospect of my going to college. Colorado takes me in the second round, 38th overall, behind Darrin Erstad, Todd Helton and Roy Halladay, and 11 spots ahead of Carlos Beltran.

I ask for $1 million, and eventually get $495,000 — a record for a second-round pick. I go to the Arizona Fall League, where Helton, who also played quarterback at Tennessee and started ahead of Peyton Manning, is my roommate. We do 100 push-ups and 100 sit-ups every night.

That spring, at the age of 18, I'm invited to big-league camp with the likes of Bret Saberhagen, Larry Walker, Ellis Burks, Walt Weiss, Vinny Castilla and Andres Galarraga.

By 1997, I'm the No. 62 prospect in all of baseball. I go to a football game at my old high school, and they chant my name.

In 1998, I hit 18 homers and am the No. 52 prospect in all of baseball. I meet Kellie Starkey at a Halloween party back home. She's four years younger but poised, unflappable, and special. The sort of person you meet and wonder where she's going. I'm fascinated. I write her a letter, which I have my sister, Mari Lyn, hand deliver.

That winter, my brother tells me my dad has a tremor in his right arm. My mother says he could barely hold a microphone in his hand when he was announcing a volleyball game.

In Feb. 1999, I report to spring training in the best shape of my life. We run a timed mile, which I finish in 5:35 — blazingly fast for a catcher. That season in Triple A, I out-hit every Pacific Coast League catcher by 35 points. Over one 20-game stretch, I hit .420 with six homers and 17 RBI.

Even my failures are spectacular: I hit into a triple-play sacrifice fly.

In July, I start for the U.S. team in the inaugural All Star Futures Game at Fenway Park. My teammates include Lance Berkman, Mark Mulder, Pat Burrell and Rick Ankiel.

On Sept. 1, at the age of 22, I get the call. Half of Hillsboro joins my dad for the afternoon at a local sport bar, and in my first at bat, I lace an RBI double off Jason Schmidt. I pull into second base and look up at 40,000 fans giving me a standing ovation.

The next day, the *Rocky Mountain News* writes this:

> **"In the aftermath of another bitter loss for the Colorado Rockies, this time 9-8 to the Pittsburgh Pirates after a second ninth-inning collapse by closer Dave Veres in less than 24 hours, (Rockies Farm Director) Paul Egins could not wipe the smile from his face.**

And no one in the home clubhouse could really blame him. Most of them, after all, were beaming right along with him. Never mind that their present is nothing short of depressing, that they fell to 60-75 after being swept in a series for the eighth time this season and the fourth time at Coors Field. Never mind that their manager, Jim Leyland, says he may forgo the final two seasons of his three-year, $6 million contract. In the person of Ben Petrick, there is hope for the future."

I hit .323 in 62 at bats with four home runs, including one in the bottom of the eighth inning off Mike Maddux in the first game my family sees me play in the majors. Two days later, I hit one off Dodgers ace Kevin Brown, and three days later I hit two in consecutive at bats against Diamondbacks All-Star Andy Benes.

The Rockies send me to the Arizona Fall League. I'm sitting in my apartment and typing on my computer, when I realize my left hand has a slight tremor and is trailing my right hand. I hold my hands up and wiggle my fingers, like a magician saying "Hocus, Pocus." My left hand is significantly slower.

I soon notice that on long jogs, the toes on my left foot start to cramp. I see a team doctor, who has no answers.

I go to Virginia for a rookie-development seminar Major League Baseball does for top prospects. I sit in my hotel room and weep silently as my father tells me doctors have confirmed the symptoms he's been experiencing are consistent with Parkinson's disease, a progressive illness caused principally when brain cells that release dopamine stop functioning. This disrupts the circuits in the part of the brain that regulates body movement. My mother's father had Parkinson's, and I know it's a cowardly, run-and-hide illness that takes all but your mind.

My dad says that he and my mother have tried going to Parkinson's support groups, but have a hard time relating because they're so young. He's barely 50, and the average age for Parkinson's onset is 60.

My symptoms are different from my father's — he has tremors, while I have stiffness — and I'm told the disease is not genetic. Plus, I'm so young.

Still, I know.

It's like something coming in the mail.

When I get to spring training in 2000, I notice my glove shakes when I give a target. I have trouble gripping the bat with my left hand. Doctors examine me for all the usual suspects, and all tests come back negative. I see a neurologist in Tucson who diagnoses me with a benign essential tremor.

In their 2000 Baseball Preview, *Sports Illustrated* writes this:

> **Thinking the day's workout was over, Ben Petrick turned his back on the field and started to**

put his catcher's gear in his equipment bag one afternoon this spring. That's when teammate Darren Bragg smacked a one-hopper right at Petrick, hitting him flush in the posterior. The incident was typical Petrick: The ball didn't get past him. "Ben is a great athlete. That's why his future is so bright," says manager Buddy Bell. "All he needs is experience."

Last year, Petrick hit a combined .313 with 27 home runs and 98 RBIs between Double-A Carolina and Triple-A Colorado Springs, then hit .323 in 62 at bats with Colorado. Though Brent Mayne will begin the year as the Rockies' starting catcher, it's just a matter of time before Petrick, who turns 23 on April 7, claims the job — for the next decade or so."

After a great deal of persistence, I get to see a movement disorder specialist in Denver who diagnoses me with "Parkinsonism." I seem too young for even young-onset Parkinson's, which accounts for 5 percent of all cases — and classic young onset usually involves a diagnosis around age 40.

"Time will tell," the doctor says. "If it gets worse, then you likely have Parkinson's disease." I'm given a drug called Requip, which I'm warned could cause nausea and exhaustion.

I return to the clubhouse, where I tell my roommate, Brent Butler, about the diagnosis. I'm quickly taken aside by someone on the medical staff: You might not want to say that too loud, he tells me. It could put a lot of things in jeopardy.

So begins my life of deceit — an existence that includes massive lies I tell myself each day. I don't go back to see a doctor for two years. I immerse myself in baseball, totally and completely.

I hit .315 in Triple-A, with a 23-game hit streak. I play in the 2000 All-Star Futures Game, where I collect the first RBI in American team history. My teammates include Josh Hamilton, Vernon Wells, Barry Zito, C.C. Sabathia, Ben Sheets and Josh Beckett.

I get called up to the big club again. On Aug. 30, at Veterans Stadium in Philadelphia, Brent Mayne challenges me to hit a go-ahead home run in the 11th inning. I tell him I will, and I do.

As I run around the bases, I tell myself to move my left arm normally. Going into the dugout, I have to make a concerted effort when giving high fives with my left hand.

On Sept. 20, I set a big-league record, getting four RBI without a hit. I pull it off with two groundouts with a runner at third, a sacrifice fly, and a bases-loaded walk. That same game, I totally whiff on catching a 93-mph fastball from Jamie Navarro.

Meanwhile, the Requip is sapping my energy. I catch pitchers in the bullpen and fight off yawns. Players are doing anything to get an edge — including steroids, human-growth hormone and amphetamines (none of which I took) — and I am nearly asleep, playing with 65-percent use of my left arm, and 30 percent use of my left hand.

By 2001, the rigidity and slowness of movement on my left side is all consuming. I have to start thinking about what clothes to buy: fewer buttons, more zippers and elastic pants. When I put on my jersey, I pull it over my head rather than buttoning it up. Opening bottles of water is nearly impossible. The stress of hiding my symptoms from my family and girlfriend — who I won't allow to hold my left hand — is becoming oppressive.

Legendary Cardinals play-by-play man Jack Buck has Parkinson's, and comes to our locker room while in the full throes of dyskinesia, the involuntary movements often caused by medications used to offset the disease.

"Is that going to be me?" I ask myself.

Miraculously, I make the big-league roster out of spring training for the first time. I hit 11 bombs that year, including one in June off Randy Johnson. I look at the tape after the game and see that as I circled the bases, my left arm was out of sync with my right.

The team trades Mayne in late June to give me a shot at the full-time catching job, which coincides precisely with a rapid escalation of my symptoms.

In July, the *Denver Post* writes this:

> **Temperatures climbed into the 90s Saturday morning, making it a good day for a swim. Come to think about it, that's what the Colorado Rockies hoped Ben Petrick would be doing — going swimmingly in his role as starting catcher.**
>
> **That hasn't happened. Petrick, shading himself in the dugout, admitted that it all hasn't sunk in yet.**
>
> **"To be honest, I guess it's just the responsibility, trying to deal with pitch calling and receiving and trying to hit and dealing with all the different things that go into catching," Petrick said. "I'm playing more often. I need to do a better job of it. I'm feeling that."**

I refuse to believe Parkinson's is causing any of my problems. The more I feel my abilities slip, the harder I work, hitting the weight room 4-5 nights a week after games.

One night I'm coming out of the shower and cross paths with a teammate. "Dude," he says. "You're ripped. Are you juicin'?"

"If you only knew what I'm on," I think to myself.

I go on the disabled list in August.

When I come back in September, I am no longer the catcher of the future.

I make the team in 2002, but struggle early. Buddy Bell is fired, Clint Hurdle takes over and I get sent down in early May to learn how to play outfield. I go to the neurologist for the first time in two years, and am taken off Requip in favor of Sinemet. I notice a major difference and start hitting again, earning another call up as an outfielder and catcher.

I have stretches during games where my medication wears off. Playing left field at PNC Park in Pittsburgh, a ground ball is hit to me and I can't open my glove to field it.

When I get back to the dugout, a teammate says, "You just need to open your glove more," as though I'm in Little League.

Larry Walker asks me if I'm hurt, because I have a slight limp. My left arm becomes rigid, and Greg Norton teases me that when I walk, it looks like I'm carrying luggage.

I can now see my glove hand quake as I give a target. On one occasion, I find it nearly impossible to remove my hitter's shin guard after a double.

Chris Singleton slides into home and spikes my forearm, which causes my left hand to shake uncontrollably. The trainers try to remove my catcher's glove. I refuse.

I take a pitch off the helmet, and come frighteningly close to blowing my cover in the concussion test. The doctor asks me to put my hands out in front of me, spread my fingers and touch my nose. I realize I can't spread the fingers on my left hand. When the doc isn't looking, I use my right hand to spread them manually.

The press is killing me. It's suggested that my weakness is between the ears — that I can't take the mental burden of the big leagues. I say nothing to dissuade them.

Meanwhile, I keep Sinemet pills in my pocket and pop them in my mouth like sunflower seeds.

Standing in the outfield, my mind wanders as I take stock of the odds:

The odds of being a once-in-a-generation athlete in the area where I grew up.

The odds of being one of the excruciatingly few who experience Parkinson's onset *nearly 40 years* earlier than average.

The odds of a father and son both having Parkinson's when there is no known genetic biomarker for the disease, and the odds of us being diagnosed just seven months apart.

The astronomical odds against all these storylines convening in one human being.

I used to feel uncommonly blessed. Now I begin to think maybe God doesn't have the slightest clue what to do with me.

By 2003, my medication intake has become absolutely reckless. I keep my pills in my right pocket, because if I go "off" — meaning my medication ceases to work sooner than I expect — I won't be able to use my left hand to get them out. I check the stadium clock constantly:

"Gary Sheffield's up. Play him to pull. It's 2 p.m. Time to take my meds."

At the All-Star Break, the Rockies trade me to the Tigers, a team on its way to losing 119 games, more than any club in American League history. My medication begins to cause some dyskinesia, and my swing is a mess. I watch video of an at bat where I go the opposite way on C.C. Sabathia, and see my left leg spasm as the ball arrives.

When the season ends, Detroit asks me to play in the Winter League. I turn it down because I know my body can't withstand this heedless onslaught of medicine much longer. I know this means my time with the team is short.

In 2004, I go to big-league camp and get sent down to Triple A Toledo with the first cuts. I'm tired of hiding, tired of taking pills, tired of poor performances. I collect no hits in my first 10 at bats, with seven strikeouts, and the Tigers release me.

I feel sweet, sweet relief.

I begin the cross-country drive home to Oregon. I talk with my agent, who urges me to reconsider. I give him a thread-the-needle scenario: The only place I'll play is with San Diego's Triple-A club in Portland.

He calls me back an hour later.

"You won't believe this, but Thad Bozied broke his leg. Portland needs a first baseman."

When I arrive in town, the *Portland Tribune* writes this:

> **The Rockies called Ben Petrick one of their best prospects and their catcher of the future. But something got in the way of greatness: competition. Petrick got his chance with the Rockies but couldn't hit consistently, and he lost his confidence throwing. Amazing, really, how somebody could be an exceptional catcher at the prep level and then lose it.**
>
> **"All the information you take in as a catcher, the game plans, the scouting reports on every hitter, calling games — I felt like I was in over my head," Petrick says. "And it hurt my offense."**

I hit a home run in my first at bat for the Beavers, with my friends and family in attendance. After a month, I retire. Even as I say the words for the first time, and tell the world I have Parkinson's, I refuse to confess to its impact. Anyone with common sense knows the ravages a disease like this must inflict on an athlete, but I'm resolutely in denial.

The *Denver Post* writes this:

> **DENVER — Ben Petrick, a 27-year-old catcher who once played for the Colorado Rockies, announced his retirement from baseball this week**

and disclosed he has been diagnosed with Parkinson's disease.

Petrick said he doesn't believe the problem had affected his physical ability but it had taken a mental toll.

"I was not enjoying playing as much as I used to," he said. "I began to wonder if it was worth the time and medication. I felt it is time to step back and reorganize my life. I still love the game, but I don't love playing it as much. I have other things I want to do."

Petrick was a second-round draft choice by Colorado in 1995. He appeared in 197 games for the Rockies from 1999 to 2003, hitting .264. He was traded to Detroit last July and was released by the Tigers this season.

Petrick said he was diagnosed with Parkinson's disease after the 1999 season. He said he plans to go to college and coach at the high school or college level.

Petrick's father also suffers from Parkinson's disease.

Former Detroit teammate Brandon Inge shared a house with Petrick this spring and had no idea of his condition.

"He's one of my best friends in baseball, and he didn't say a thing," Inge said. "Either he was very embarrassed about the whole situation or he didn't want to burden anyone with a feeling of guilt."

People are shocked. In so many words I try to tell them, "I'm still here. I'm still here."

But I'm not. The small part of me that was Parkinson's is now all of me. There's no air between the me and the disease.

I tell my parents I'm not sure I should marry Kellie given my condition. My mother says, "She's a very smart girl. You should let her decide that."

I ask, and Kellie accepts. We're married on Makena Beach on Maui.

The years pass. I try college. I try coaching. My health continues to get worse, with my downturn accelerated by the massive quantity of medicine I took in my playing days. When I go "off," I feel as if I'm encased in cement. I am constantly fatigued, as though I've spent the day digging ditches. I become anxious in crowds. I have a strange resistance to walking through doorways. I've lost 20 pounds, but refuse to eat during the day for fear it will negatively affect my medication.

I can't bring myself to go on the sidelines during football games; instead, I stay in the announcer's booth and run the video camera. Some nights, my buddy Erik has to do it for me.

My doctor can't fathom how I played parts of five major league seasons with this condition. A writer likens it to swimming the English Channel while someone throws deck chairs at you.

I have an office dedicated to proof of life: old jerseys, signed baseballs and pictures from my playing days. I add a new photo with a brief inscription:

> **Ben and Kellie,**
>
> **We're going to get this done.**
>
> **All my best,**
>
> **Michael J. Fox**

All my life, I've dreamed of being a dad. In 2007, we have Makena, our beautiful daughter.

The thing is, I didn't dream of being a "sometimes" father; one who is there at times, and other times has to sit it out. I have a giant of a father, and I want to be at least as good. But I'm forced to adjust, and accept I'll be less than I dreamed.

We move onto the lane where I grew up, the same one I sprinted down as I ran from my brother. We get a house across the street from where my parents live so that my mother, when she's not caring for my dad, can help me with

Makena. Meanwhile, Kellie goes back to work as a third-grade teacher. I go on disability.

My symptoms get even worse.

Every time Makena enters a room, I take mental snapshots of her. She might just be putting on a shoe, but I want to suspend the moment in my mind.

Every time Kellie enters a room, I want to ask, "Wouldn't you be happier with someone else?" But I don't ask. I don't want to know the answer.

I'm overcome by a sadness that seems to be the very definition of the word: To look at a woman and a child, and love them madly, desperately, deeply — and at the same time think I'm hurting them with my very presence.

This is where the heartbreak starts …

And this is where the prologue stops.

**

This is when the pages start to matter.

This is where my talents, my town, my family — all of the things I did not choose — can no longer provide the answers.

This is where I take part in my survival.

This is where I come to a deep-down understanding of the spirit within me.

This is where I take control.

This is where I fight.

I've gone from playing in front of 40,000 screaming fans to an audience of one.

And she needs her dad.

THE ASTRONAUT

My father was the oldest boy among 15 siblings, which his mother had by four different men. Vern Petrick grew up in Klamath Falls, a fallow, one-time timber town with no actual waterfalls. Portland was more than five hours away by car back then — and when it snowed, Portland may as well have not existed.

Twenty miles from the California line, Klamath Falls was and remains a frontier town. Main Street looks like the set for "A Fistful of Dollars," and life revolves around places like the Leatherneck Club, the Shady Cove Saloon, and the Bum Steer Dance Palace.

When my dad was there, the chief export of Klamath Falls was despair. More than a quarter of the town's population, which included a big Native American community, lived beneath the poverty line.

Historians say the Klamath tribe of southern Oregon has been in the area for at least 10,000 years, making it one of the oldest and longest enduring in North America. But at the turn of the 20th century, federal Indian agents gave them "American" names, handing them legal documents the Klamaths couldn't even read.

Every generation that followed saw its children torn from their homes and sent to religious schools. In the 1950s, one local Catholic school advertised its mission as being "to take the child away from the barbaric surroundings of the teepee and … mold him in the ways of civilization." Stripped of their traditions, these kids had nothing but destitution waiting for them after graduation day.

When my dad was a boy, the federal government "terminated" the Klamaths, selling off the rich timberlands of their reservation under the pretense of integrating the tribe into mainstream society.

The Klamath Falls of that era was every bit as racially charged as the American South. At one point, Native relations boiled over into what many called an "Indian War," as Klamaths marched through town to protest mistreatment by local shopkeepers. The mayor of Klamath Falls was nonchalant about the situation, telling a reporter, "Indians as a whole — with a few exceptions — are a pretty irresponsible group."

As if that wasn't enough oppression for one place, the Klamath Basin was also home to the largest internment camp for Japanese-Americans during World War II, with nearly 18,000 detained against their will.

Even Klamath Falls' one natural wonder is a symbol of the area's false promise. Upper Klamath Lake, which is 20 miles long and eight miles wide at some points, is the largest body of water in Oregon. At its deepest, though, the lake is barely four feet.

It seems appropriate the species most seen in those waters is the suckerfish.

My dad grew up in appalling squalor and neglect, sharing a filthy 500-square-foot shanty that had no indoor plumbing with his mother, brothers and sisters. The smallest of the children slept in bureau drawers. Each day my dad wore the same clothes, which he tried to clean before school with a wet rag. He didn't have his own toothbrush until he was 18. One of the main reasons he went out for sports in junior high was so he could take a shower after practice.

My dad wasn't even born in a hospital — in fact, his first visit to the doctor came when he was 5 or 6, and it resulted in a scar he still has on his neck today from where he was given an emergency tracheotomy. He had diphtheria, a bacterial infection that was rarely seen in the U.S., where doctors had been immunizing against it for years. To save his life, thick green mucous had to be dug out of his throat to clear his airway.

My dad and his siblings were constantly malnourished. Not much grows in the marshy earth and muck soils of Klamath Falls, save for dry onions and potatoes — lots and lots of potatoes. My dad says he ate raw potato sandwiches for breakfast, lunch and dinner.

My mom remembers that the first time she visited the house where my dad grew up, the younger siblings were sitting on a couch near the front door. When the kids stood up to hug him, mice scurried out from under the cushions.

My parents met in college — yes, college.

As unlikely as a flower growing in the desert, my dad made it to Southern Oregon University, where he got his degree in education and played football. He eventually became a high school coach and athletic director, and a leader in our church and community. Despite figuring out how to be a father on the fly, he was a great one. He was like a guy who'd never seen a piano, but put his fingers on the keys for the first time and was a virtuoso.

Somehow he was a tomorrow person. To cover the distance he did — to go from the hellish world where he was born to the one he made for us — my dad might as well have built a rocket and gone to the moon. He was for all intents and purposes an astronaut.

My mom was raised on a turkey farm in Oregon City. Her upbringing was happy, but far from lavish. With my parents' combined backgrounds, it's not surprising that conservation was a theme in our house.

I have one specific memory of when I was about four years old, and I made myself breakfast for the first time. I put bread in the toaster, and then realized there wasn't any butter left. So I did what I'd seen my mother do a number of times. I went in the refrigerator and grabbed a new cube of butter. I removed the paper around it and put the cube on a plate. Then I took a knife and scraped every ounce of remaining butter off the paper, and spread it on my toast.

Just then my mother came into the room and gave me the most glowing smile. She was so proud that I'd used every last bit of what we'd paid for.

A few years later, we moved into our house in Hillsboro, which my parents essentially built themselves. During construction, they cut extra wood to warm the house in the cold months so we could save on the heating bill.

But as winter persisted, my folks realized the wood we'd cut wouldn't be enough. Fortunately, a home was being built next door, and the contractor said we could take the oak trees he'd cut down so long as we chopped the wood and hauled it.

It was well below freezing outside. Still, my dad bundled me up and took me to help him. We opened our back door and walked across the deck he had made by hand, then across the lawn he'd planted. We found our way to the fallen trees.

My job was to hold the limbs steady while my dad cut — not a difficult task in the slightest. I lasted a short while, but then grew cold and impatient. I complained a little, and then a lot. Eventually my dad looked at me dismissively and said, "Just go inside, Ben. If it's too much for you to handle, just go inside. I can do it myself."

So I walked back across the grass he'd grown and the deck he'd made, and stepped into the house he'd built that was warmed by wood he'd cut.

I took off my coat and sat in the window for hours, watching my dad work alone in the freezing cold.

And I thought to myself, "That's what a man is."

TITLETOWN

There's a line I'm scared to cross.

It won't be long before I'll have had Parkinson's for as many years as I didn't have it, and soon after that my healthy years will be in the minority. The portion of my life when I was physically whole was focused almost entirely on sports. Sometimes I'm bothered by the idea that those days revolved around events and accomplishments which in the end may have been inconsequential.

Did any of it matter?

I specifically wonder about our football team's glorious march to the Oregon state championship in 1994. The absence of real-world concerns back then made those emotions feel especially potent, to the extent that even now I can access them at a moment's notice. But knowing what I do now, I can't help but contemplate if those feelings are just fool's gold.

These days, Hillsboro is an ever-expanding tech hub that is home to major offices for the likes of Yahoo!, Sun Microsystems and Intel. Some call it the "Silicon Forest." So to be clear, we are not talking about Odessa, Tex., the setting for the book *Friday Night Lights*, where they "only have two things — football and oil, and there ain't no more oil." In present-day Hillsboro, if football went away for some reason, it would be far from the end of everything.

This wasn't always the case.

It's hard to believe that less than two decades ago, the area was mostly farmland, geographically situated 30 minutes outside of Portland, but seemingly 30 hours from everywhere. That version of Hillsboro was the sort of place where a tradition could take hold and unite everyone in a little end-of-the-week euphoria.

When he coached at Notre Dame, Lou Holtz said of game days in South Bend, "If you've been there, no explanation is necessary. If you haven't, none is adequate."

The same could have been said back then about Hillsboro in the fall. There was no other topic of conversation besides high school football. You were either for Glencoe, where my father was athletic director, or "Hill" High. There was no in between.

On our side of town, Crimson Tide football was an institution that extended well beyond school grounds. You signed up for Glencoe Youth Football in second grade and ran the same plays on a continuous loop through your senior year, with the same buddies doing the handing off and the blocking.

My brother, Rian, and I were ball boys for the first Glencoe team to win a state title in 1986. From that moment forward, we and every other boy in our neighborhood grew up dreaming of dressing out for the Tide.

When it came to sports, my brother was a god to me — sometimes a vengeful god, but supernatural nonetheless. As his baby brother by four years, I basked in reflected glory as Rian became Glencoe's starting quarterback. His games remained the heartbeat of our family activity even after he graduated and went to nearby Linfield College to play football and baseball.

It takes two men to make a brother. Unfortunately, we were just boys then, and I determinedly refused to let Rian know how I felt. All marvel and awe was conducted in the total privacy of my mind. Like all brothers, we buried our love under layers of rivalry, jealousies and posturing, defining ourselves more by our differences than our similarities. We kept one another in our periphery after Rian left for college, constantly aware but rarely speaking.

My senior year, our team was 13-0 and set to face undefeated Marshfield for the state title at University of Oregon's Autzen Stadium.

When I returned home from practice a couple days before the game, there was a letter addressed to me on the kitchen counter. I looked at the return address and saw my brother's name. Inside was a card, with a picture of a dog swimming with a rope in its teeth. In Rian's handwriting, it read:

Ben,

Win, lose, or draw this weekend, you've had a
spectacular season. You've suffered through all
the hard work that it takes to get where you
are. You're the man for the Crimson Tide. All
year long you've lead and the team has learned by
your actions. Go out there Saturday and play
within yourself. Do your job. When and if things
don't your way, be the one with "the
Rope." Throw the rope out and let your
teammates grab on. Then pull them all together.

If you can't tell I'm a little pumped up for this
game. All of Linfield is behind you. **MAKE IT
HAPPEN!**

R.P

We did win, 28-17, in a game that was televised statewide. All
heaven broke loose. When we returned to Hillsboro, the
team climbed aboard fire engines that drove us through the
Glencoe side of town. It seemed like every business had a
sign in its window congratulating us. We ended up back at
the high school where a huge party awaited.

Inside, the game was being replayed on a TV screen at the
far end of the gym.

Getting back to my original question: Did any of it matter?

You tell me.

If you looked closely at the TV screen, you could see a guy on the sidelines racing along with me every time I touched the ball. When I ran, he ran. When I stopped, he stopped. When I fumbled, he just shouted encouragement.

It was Rian.

Sixteen years later and counting, he's still doing the same thing, in one form or another. The world might see us getting older, but to one other, we remain who we were that day.

Are you going to tell me that didn't matter?

FALLING AND FLYING

A couple interesting things happen when you're diagnosed with a serious illness.

First, people start naming things after you, like ball fields and babies. (Tremendous honors, both.)

Second, things get very, very quiet.

And quiet is particularly unsettling for an honorary Blues Brother.

When I was drafted by the Rockies out of high school in 1995, I'd barely been on an airplane. So it was overwhelming to say the least when, as I was hitting Whiffle balls with my dad in our backyard, I received a phone call from the team requesting that I report to big-league camp when I got to spring training. I was still 18, but for at least a few days, my teammates would be guys like Larry Walker, Andres Galarraga and Vinny Castilla.

Fortunately, I was a veteran little brother. I knew the rules.

Rule #1: Before all else, humble yourself.

After I arrived at the Tucson facility, I had to ask a reporter named Mike Klis to point me to the clubhouse. The first player I came across was Bret Saberhagen, the two-time Cy Young Award winner and MVP of the 1985 World Series. He was coming off a shoulder injury and was rehabbing in the training room.

"Hi," he said, extending his hand. "I'm Bret."

"I know," I said. I'd come prepared, and fished his baseball card out of my bag. "Could I have your autograph?"

Rule #2: Get to the joke before they do

My next stop was Asheville, S.C., where the vast majority of my teammates were at least four years older than I was. Someone put Vanilla Ice on the clubhouse stereo, and dressed in nothing but a towel, I jumped into a full-on dance routine that was a mash-up of about six boy bands at once. Guys were howling, and the dance became a daily clubhouse ritual.

I was kind of a mascot that year, with the older players taking it upon themselves to corrupt the country boy and his Methodist sensibilities. My roommate was Jason Dietrich, who'd been a star pitcher at Pepperdine University in Malibu. On my own, my diet would have included two food groups: donuts and Mountain Dew. Dietrich did all he could to introduce two new ones: Bud and Coors.

John Hallead, an outfielder and fellow Northwesterner from Ellensburg, Wash., took to calling me Fred, because he thought I looked like the character from "Scooby-Doo."

"Fred," he'd say, "Chipper Jones might be chipper, but you're the happiest guy I've ever been around."

In minor-league ballparks, they bring in different acts to help sell tickets. One of the classics was the Blues Brothers, with two guys dressed in the suits, dark glasses and hats like Dan Ackroyd and John Belushi wore in the movie. They even had the old police car Jake and Elwood drove to go see The Penguin. During the seventh-inning stretch, these guys pulled me out of the dugout and I did a whole routine with them.

Rule #3: Don't think. Just fall.

After my first full season in Asheville, the Rockies sent me to Maui for two months to play in the Aloha League, where my teammates included Josh Booty, who'd received a record signing bonus from the Marlins and later quarterbacked at LSU, and Mark Kotsay, who'd just won a national title at Cal-State Fullerton and been named the Most Outstanding Player of the College World Series.

We all had ravenous appetites for life — the sort of guys about whom Kerouac may have been referring when he wrote of people "desirous of everything at the same time … Who burn, burn, burn like Roman candles across the night."

Nine miles south of Hana are the Seven Sacred Pools, natural swimming holes networked by a series of waterfalls.

We'd pile in a Jeep and drive to the pools on the rare days when we had free time.

Sunsets from atop the falls looked like they'd been finger painted — not that I had much time to look at them. My buddies were waiting for me down below, and without thinking, I stepped off the ledge to join them, yelping all the way down.

It was the sound a person makes when he doesn't have a care in the world and is blessedly free of insight.

Life would soon be full of quiet, and trips of a different kind.

Sometimes when I'd stumble, I'd close my eyes, and remember what it felt like to just fall.

FLUSH

Big-league baseball has a secret the marketing guys don't want you to know:

The players you see on the field are not necessarily the most talented in the world.

This is because baseball is a game of failure. For this reason, surviving relies on something more important than talent, and that's grit.

You might be surprised how many ungodly athletes make it to pro ball, only to pack their bags the second they realize they're going to have to fight if they want to remain the guy they read about in their hometown newspaper.

All excellence requires deliberate practice. The willingness to practice hour after hour, day after day, requires humility — which is in short supply among star athletes.

There was a study done recently on kids competing in the National Spelling Bee. Researchers found the kids who scored lower on standard IQ tests but committed more time to deliberate practice performed better than those considered more intelligent who practiced less. The gritty high performers were those willing to practice often and alone.

To be a great writer, you must enjoy writing, and not just having written. To be devout, you must enjoy the act of praying, and not just having prayed. You have to see the value in the process before you see the value in the recognition. The process has to be the real currency of your life.

Grit, then, is your essential self. It's who you are when you're left with nothing but the air in your lungs and a decision to make. Can you accept you have work to do? Are you willing to be seen as imperfect?

This did not always describe me.

If you asked my childhood teammates what they remember about me from our early years, I'm sure they'd mention my tendency to cry. It was pretty much an every-game deal. I came into the world hard-wired with a relentless longing to be perfect and successful — or at least appear to be. Anything less than perfection caused me to explode into tears.

This personality flaw swelled inside me as I grew older, and by the time I reached pro ball, narcissism had filled every corner of my being. Whenever I struggled, I wondered, "How must this look to others? What will others think of me when they find out I've failed?" The foundation of my psyche was built on sand.

I hit .175 my first month as a professional — more that 500 points below the average I'd maintained most of my senior year. I'd call my parents almost nightly, complaining and near tears because I wasn't sure I could handle pro ball.

This temperament would hold me back from the big leagues for a long time. At least once a month I would have a blow up and take a bat to the chairs in the locker room. The thought that kept running through my mind was, "What must everyone think of me?"

Many baseball people said I was ready to catch in the big leagues at the age of 20. But as my fourth minor-league season began, I was still in Double A and going through the worst defensive stretch of my career. After one particularly horrendous game, I refused to go in the clubhouse because I knew that if I did, I'd probably march into the manager's office and quit.

I'd always been a spiritual guy, though for previous couple years that aspect of my life had taken a backseat to more tangible signs of progress or regression (like my slugging percentage).

There's a tension between the essence of sports and the essence of faith. Sports is about winning and being supreme. Faith is about humility. To a young man, on most days the two felt incompatible.

But after this game, I walked out beyond the outfield fence, laid in the grass like a summertime snow angel, and prayed. I asked for some kind of sign as to what I should do next.

"What's up?" a voice behind me asked.

I looked up startled, and found one of my teammates standing there. I told him I didn't know if I could go on.

"You need to learn to flush," he said.

"Huh?"

"You need to find a way to flush each day and take the next one as a new one," he said. "You're too good for all this."

We talked some more, and I resolved to forget the numbers and the perceptions, and just focus on being a little better each day — on enjoying the process, not just the results. I committed to being someone I liked, rather than being someone everybody else loved. It was time to have fun. Doubt was no longer allowed to run the show.

Voltaire wrote, "Perfect is the enemy of the good." That night, I put good before perfect, and grit before talent. Who was I really? The guy I read about in newspapers, or the guy I was when I humbled myself and prayed?

As in all sports, baseball players lose statistically and get hurt physically. These pains are transitory. The only lasting pain — the thing that really aches — is the daily reckoning you have with losing your livelihood. That the game will pass you by is inevitable. That there are 10 guys in your own company who want your job is inarguable. Couple this with the fact that great hitters fail seven out of 10 times at the plate, and the game becomes mental warfare: Is a strikeout just the law of averages, or a sign that you're closer to the end of your career than the beginning?

The few who discover their grit, push back and don't allow themselves to be defined by the failures are the ones who survive the gauntlet.

Grit allows you to drive the pain of baseball back to arm's length. It allows you to recognize that an 0-for-5 day that hints at certain doom is not fact, but fiction.

Faith and sport don't entirely contradict, because they both require courage and patience (and the understanding that it takes courage to be patient).

I went back to my manager, Jay Loviglio, and asked him to please keep me in the lineup. I hit for the cycle the following day. The next five months I went on a tear. In just one season I jumped to Triple A, and then to the big leagues.

We've all seen the athlete who hangs on too long and plays one season too many: Willie Mays with the Mets; Joe Namath with the Rams; Michael Jordan with the Wizards. There's a chance I'd have been no different. Athletes do this because we're scared we'll have no value away from sports. Our production on the field has been the currency of our lives. Without sports, will we be poor?

Baseball did me a favor by stripping me bare and revealing my true grit, because just two months after my big-league call-up I experienced my first Parkinson's symptoms. Soon I'd be out of the game and back home, raw, scorched and cleansed of every affectation. I was facing the same decision I did that night lying in the grass:

Do I quit, or do I keep going?

Fortunately, just in the nick of time, I'd learned I was valuable apart from the game. With or without baseball, whether I could hear the applause or not, I was rich and not poor. Grit was my currency, not talent.

No longer worried about being perfect, I was brought closer to good.

UP

I got the call."

I'd been waiting to utter those words my entire life. And on Aug. 31, 1999, standing at a gas station along Colorado's I-25 headed north toward Denver, I finally got to say them to my parents.

"I got the call," I said. "I'll be in the big leagues tomorrow."

Earlier that day, Bill Hayes, our manager at Triple A Colorado Springs, announced in front of the team that Luther Hackman (an unfortunate name for a pitcher) and I were getting called up by the Rockies. I'd ended up having a breakthrough season, hitting.311 with 23 HR and 86 RBI. Every major scouting service had me as the No. 1 catching prospect in baseball. The migration of prospects to their parent clubs happens every year when rosters expand on Sept. 1, and Luther and I were moving.

I told my parents I loved them and jumped in my truck. The skies were clear where I was standing, but I could see there were thunderstorms forming over Denver.

When I reached the city, I checked into my hotel room, which overlooked a lit-up Coors Field brimming with fans. Starting the next day, it would be my office.

I got to the ballpark at 8 a.m. for a 1p.m. day game. I pounded on the doors until a clubby finally let me in. I'd woken him up, as the game the night before hadn't ended until 1 in the morning because of the rain.

"You don't need to be here for three hours," he said, rubbing his eyes.

But I wasn't going anywhere. He gave in, leading me down the tunnel to the huge clubhouse and a locker with "PETRICK" on the nameplate above it. I noticed my new manager, the legendary Jim Leyland, asleep on a fold out in his office. In a bit of foreshadowing, his wife never moved to Denver, so Leyland took to sleeping at the park.

Teammates eventually started trickling in, wearily going about their day-game routine. It had been an unusually harsh season, with the club scoring runs in bunches, but giving them up just as quickly. They were 15 games under .500, and Leyland, arguably the finest skipper in the game and just two years removed from winning a totally improbable World Series in Florida, was in his first — and last — season as manager.

It had just been a strange year for the team overall. The Rockies played their home opener in Monterrey, Mexico, of all places. Two weeks later, the horrific Columbine High massacre occurred nearby and the team had taken a leadership role in helping the community begin to heal. And ten days before I arrived, Bob Gebhard, who had been the only general manager in the franchise's history, announced his resignation and was replaced by Dan O'Dowd.

All in all, it had been a grind for the guys, and the corrosive effect of a year spent losing in all respects was evident in the slow machinery of their legs.

At long last, the lineup card was posted on the wall closest to the door leading out to the field. I eased my way over to it, moving at about one-thousandth the speed of my racing heart.

It read:

1. Neifi Perez, SS
2. Terry Schumpert, 2B
3. Larry Walker, RF
4. Dante Bichette, LF
5. Vinny Castilla, 3B
6. Todd Helton, 1B
7. Jeff Barry, CF
8. Ben Petrick, C
9. Luther Hackman, P

It was official. I was 22 and the catcher for the Colorado Rockies, leaning fearlessly into my future. There was not a single cell in my body that felt I wouldn't be checking this board for the next 15 years.

My first at bat came in the second inning with Helton at second. The pitcher was Pirates ace Jason Schmidt. I ran the count to 3-and-1, got the fastball I was sitting on, and lined it into the gap for an RBI double. I cruised into second base standing up.

Forty thousand fans stood and cheered. That wall of sound was so dense I could've hung a picture on it. But I didn't smile.

I thought moments like these would stretch on until I told them to stop. This isn't to say I took the moment for granted. But never in my life did I seriously think it wouldn't happen. When I was young, I'd challenge any kid to any physical test: jump the highest hedge, race the block, whatever. It never occurred to me I might lose. It never occurred to me there might be a day when I'd lose the magical ability to make your jaw drop.

Now 40,000 fans had their eyes on me, enjoying the pure possibility I represented.

Two months later, I experienced my first Parkinson's symptoms.

It wasn't long before my anxiety was so far off the charts that I begged Clint Hurdle, our hitting instructor at the time, to tell our manager he should send me to the minors.

It wasn't long before I fell into an 0-for-23 slump.

It wasn't long before Leyland's replacement, Buddy Bell — as decent a man as I ever met in baseball — was calling me into his office to say not to worry, that he wasn't going to send me back to the minors.

It wasn't long before I was sitting in a booth at the back of a steakhouse adjacent to Coors Field with Larry Walker, one of my favorite players as a teenager, who calmly explained that detachment was an essential part of the job. You survive by being a little dead inside.

It wasn't long before I'd have traded places with any of those 40,000 souls who on that perfect September day were unified in wondering where I was going.

For all it took, though, Parkinson's did give me one thing: a total presence in every moment.

It wasn't long before I'd have all the insight in the world on how to live, yet be powerless to act on it. (Such is the paradox of illness that our wisdom and toothlessness seem to grow in inverse proportion.) But for a little while, I stood perfectly at the intersection of understanding and empowerment.

I played 240 games in the big leagues — all but 19 with the knowledge I had Parkinson's disease. Because of this, I never developed that calcified indifference some athletes often take on. I answered every reporter's question thoughtfully. I signed every autograph. I sat alone in the locker room and committed every detail to memory. I lived in an "other" space that was all my own — a fan as well as a player.

Anticipating a day when the feeling might be gone from my hands and arms, I committed to memory the kinesthetic joy of feeling *nothing* on those rare occasions when ball and bat aligned perfectly.

When we traveled, most guys would stay in their rooms until game time, playing video games or watching movies. But I always felt I might never get back to those cities, so I'd go walking by myself. If you asked me, I could describe to you the architecture of Constitution Hall, the crack in the Liberty Bell, or Elvis Presley's bedroom. I walked through the cornfields of Iowa and the steel mills of Pittsburgh like they were South Beach and Las Vegas. I stared at nothing at Ground Zero and in Oklahoma City.

I knew in my heart that my ability to play the game was a gift, not a promise. It was something given to me in a moment of grace.

Still, I couldn't help but close my eyes and ask ...

Please give me one more town.

One more game.

One more day.

SAY IT LOUD

I left the doctor's office wondering what the appropriate response should be to finding out you're just 22 and no longer free from time.

A doctor at University Hospital in Denver had told me the odd movement disorders I'd been experiencing for nearly six months were caused by "Parkinsonism" — he said he would have diagnosed me with actual Parkinson's disease, but I was four decades younger than the typical patient.

Getting that diagnosis (just seven months after my father received the same news) was more than surreal. It was like watching the moon fall.

I walked silently to my truck, put the key in the ignition, and merged onto I-25 South to make my way back to Colorado Springs, where in May 2000 I was with the Rockies Triple-A club.

That's when a beige Volvo cut me off. I put my blinker on, pulled to the side of the highway, and turned off the engine.

I cried for one minute.

Then I merged back into civilization. I wouldn't see a doctor again for two years. I wouldn't cry again for five.

And based on advice I got when I arrived back at the clubhouse, I shut my mouth about my condition for fear it would jeopardize my spot on the Rockies' 40-man roster. I told no one.

Well, almost no one.

Much as the value of team is preached at baseball's highest levels, each individual is also a commodity whose value to the club is measured unemotionally. This value has to do with on-field performance, as well as your perceived worth to other teams in a potential trade. While I'm confident the Rockies would have supported me emotionally, I'm just as confident some hard decisions would have been made about my future.

My decision to keep my diagnosis below the radar can be interpreted as self-preservation or deceit, and both are equally correct. But I was raised to be a moral person, and my choice to withhold my secret kicked up an undertow that pulled me relentlessly toward a sea of massive guilt.

The ethical burden — on top of the fact that most coaches, teammates and fans saw me as a failure — sometimes became too much to take. So I'd leak the truth out, just a little. I never told the whole story, but just enough to suggest that maybe, just maybe, there was a reason for all this.

Again, these were not long, profound conversations, and I never divulged enough to make someone complicit in my deception. I've had longer talks about motor oil. But in a way I was asking, "Can you help me?" which is easily the best compliment I could give a guy.

One of the great things about sports is the people it brings into your life. I came from a sedate, rural area in Oregon's Willamette Valley. Most of my friends were just like I was: white, churchgoing and upright. But sports have an uncanny way of bringing the unknown, uncomfortable and unconfronted into your life.

When I was drafted in 1995, I'd barely been outside Oregon. Five years later, my closest friends in the game — the very few guys I let in on the reality of my life — were quite different from those I'd grown up with. Three of them — Todd Helton, Brent Butler and Mike DeJean — were as Southern as Skynrd, barbecue and Atticus Finch; another, Greg Norton, was from Oakland, swaggering and streetwise. Each conversation I had with them was as important as it was fast.

But by far the most surprising confidante was a coach who on the surface was my alter ego. Clint Hurdle is the biggest thing in every room he enters — if not physically, then simply by being larger than life. I first met him in 1995 when he was a roving hitting instructor in the Rockies chain.

You always heard Clint before you saw him. He used words like musical notes, making them rise and fall depending on the need. Clint's sonic voice would shake the clubhouse, and paired with his massive physical stature, made him seem almost as if he'd sprung from a child's imagination. The most remarkable thing about Clint was that he actually existed.

A ball club is typically made up of guys who've been stars their entire lives, with egos to match. But when Clint walked into a room, he was the thermostat, and he turned everyone else into thermometers.

When I met Clint, I was in the batting cage for my first hitting session along with five other guys. He had each of us do a very simple drill where you pick up a ball and try to hit a line drive to the back of the cage. It's harder than it sounds, and few had done it more than once until I stepped in and did it five or six times in a row.

From the back of the cage emerged a voice that sounded like it had come up a mile of dirt road. "Well," Clint cackled, "some guys are just blessed with the hitting sperm."

When he was 20, Clint was on the cover of *Sports Illustrated* alongside the headline, "This Year's Phenom." We were all too young to have seen him play, but we were aware that his career had fallen considerably short of expectations.

Coming from the orderly world I did, at first I didn't quite know what to think of the outsized Clint Hurdle. He was electric, rough around the edges, impossible to understate, a burn-the-boats leader, and quite unlike anyone I'd ever met.

So if you'd asked me after that first day in the batting cage if Clint would have been my go-to guy in a crisis, I'd have said you were crazy.

Soon enough, though, I was in desperate need of something real, as I was spending more and more of my day hiding a disease that had become as fundamental to me as the color of my eyes. I needed something authentic — and Clint was the genuine article.

That's how, in May 2000, I found myself knocking on Clint's hotel room door in the middle of the night.

I told him that anxiety was consuming me, and that I slept with the TV on so that when I inevitably woke up during the night I could quickly get away from my negative thoughts. I was already taking far-too-big doses of Requip so I could play, and I was exhausted and nauseous. I'd been called up to replace Scott Servais, who'd gotten injured. Among other things, a throwing hitch that I'd developed and largely overcome in the minors was resurfacing. The only thing I wanted was to go back to Triple-A and pull myself together.

"Everybody has demons, Ben," he said.

Then Clint displayed real grace, as he laid his own demons out without equivocation. He'd lost his career, his family and his money to substance abuse. For two decades, he was in a perpetual state of losing and recovering his faith, then losing it again.

In 1998, after dating Karla Yearick for six years, he asked her to marry him — and she said no. She told Clint that he was still trying to please too many people, instead of making himself happy.

Karla's words sparked Clint's conversion. He stopped drinking. He reaffirmed his faith. Eventually, she married him.

Sitting there, I realized we had a shocking amount in common. We were both raised in good families, and were the kind of "Johnny Prep" guys no one ever thought would have problems. Both of us were afflicted, pulled in entirely opposite directions by forces over which we seemingly had no control. We were both prisoners of our own potential.

And we both felt there must be a reason for all of it, which in time would be revealed. Clint told me I was being challenged to live an uncommon life.

I look at Clint today, raising three children (one with special needs), happily married and a true leader of men as manager of the Pittsburgh Pirates, and realize that failing to become "The Next Phenom" opened a door to something bigger in his life.

Looking at him then, sitting in his hotel room as the sun rose, I had an inkling that removing his disguises and telling his story out loud was what Clint was born to do. Life is a strange calculus, and this was clearly a man who had arrived at the "equals" sign.

I got what I needed from our Clint that night, as I suspect many of his players have in the years since. Just as some singers can hit notes but they don't hit us, coaches can talk a lot but have no meaning. That night, Clint was the genuine article, every bit as soulful and authentic as Otis Redding, Al Green or Sam Cooke. He didn't just talk — he told the truth. There could be no separating him from his music.

I sleep a bit better now, and when I do, I often have baseball dreams. In some I win; in others I lose — but Clint finds his way into most of them, always rooting for me.

And doing it loudly.

INDIVISIBLE

On Sept. 9, 2001, at Coors Field, Barry Bonds hit three home runs, numbers 61, 62 and 63, on his way to a single-season record of 73. The first one traveled almost 500 feet and took our clubhouse attendants 30 minutes to find at the bottom of a fountain. Bonds was far from San Francisco and a mile above sea level, but still managed a "splash hit." I was in disbelief.

I'd soon learn the true meaning of that word.

Two days later in Phoenix, I woke up to my cell phone ringing. It was a beautiful morning, though I had no way of knowing that, because like all ballplayers, I had the shades in my hotel room drawn tight. On travel days, I would turn the temperature on cool, snuggle up in the warm blankets, and sleep until 10:00 or 11:00 a.m.

We'd arrived in Phoenix at 2:00 a.m. so I wanted to make sure I got my eight hours of sleep before heading to the ballpark. Getting a phone call at 8:30 when you're on the road feels like 4 a.m. does to a person who works normal hours — and nothing good comes from those type of calls.

Kellie was on the other end of the line. She was telling me to turn on the TV.

"It doesn't matter what channel," she said.

 I sat up and watched what unfolded that horrific day, Sept. 11, 2001.

I called my teammates, Todd Helton, Jeff Cirillo, Brent Butler and Greg Norton, and we gathered in a hotel room wondering what would happen next, not just to baseball, but to the world.

We all wanted to get home, but the airlines had been shut down. We talked about taking a bus north to Denver, but after three days we were cleared for a private flight.

Major League Baseball set Sept. 17 as the date for us to return to the field. On television, there was considerable debate about whether or not professional sports should resume their seasons.

That first game back left no doubt as to the answer. Baseball is a deeply American game, and never was that truer than that night in Denver, which was the most awe-inspiring thing I experienced in my sporting career.

For a typical game, there are tens of thousands of fans and just 25 players per side, so the relationship tends to be one-sided.

But I'll never forget taking that first step out of the dugout, only to feel like I was being carried toward the field on a wave. I turned to see thousands of American flags in the air; with every voice crying, "U-S-A! U-S-A!"

I looked in the stands, and this time I saw each face. Some were crying, some were hopeful, some had their faces buried in the chests of loved ones. All were counting on us to give them three hours of communion, where each person could be in a space with like-minded individuals, forgetting and remembering at the same time. The fans had been there for us game after game. This was a chance for us to be there for them, so they might lay their burdens down for a few hours. We were all one, fused together in a muscular empathy.

In the middle of the seventh inning, a time traditionally reserved for "Take Me Out To The Ballgame," our team and the Diamondbacks came together in the middle of the infield, held a huge American flag and sang "God Bless America" along with the crowd.

"Disbelief" doesn't do that moment justice.

"Belief" does the job, though.

FAR FROM HOME

Have you ever had one of those stark moments where you realize you've become a funhouse-mirror version of the man you used to be?

Telling off Kirk Gibson qualified as such a moment for me.

My parents were both educators, and my father was also an athletic director. There was no greater compliment in our world than to call someone "Coach." That title was sacrosanct in the Petrick home.

When I signed with the Rockies in 1995, as luck would have it the club's Single-A affiliate was based in Portland. I signed too late to play in games, but I was able to practice with the club at the end of their season.

My first day, I drove down to PGE Stadium in downtown Portland, parking in the fan lot a few blocks away, just as I had my entire life. I threw my high school catching gear in my bag, slung it over my shoulder, and started walking.

About a block from the stadium, a truck pulled up. The window rolled down halfway, just enough so I could see a pair of kind eyes peering out.

"Where you going?" the driver asked.

"The ballpark, sir," I answered.

"What's your name?"

"Ben Petrick, sir."

The door swung open.

"I'm P.J. Carey," he said, identifying himself as the manager of the team. "I'll drive you."

He looked me up and down. I was grimy from working at a family friend's new golf course all day.

"Normally we wear a collared shirt to the park," he said. "And you probably shouldn't be working out in the sun all day. You need to save your strength. Baseball's your job now."

"I'm sorry about all this, sir," I said.

"That's O.K.," he said, grinning. "You've got some time to learn."

P.J. would later be my manager in 1996 with the Asheville Tourists. He was the first in a succession of very good men for whom I had the chance to play, including Don Baylor, Jim Leyland, Buddy Bell and Clint Hurdle. I've known P.J. for almost 17 years now, and through good times and bad, his suggesting that I had time is the only incorrect thing he's ever said to me.

One of the cruelest things about Parkinson's is the collateral damage it does beyond your physical health. It might freeze your body, but your mind still races. You're left to watch the world go by, not knowing how or when to engage. You start to feel like an opportunity cost to everyone in your world. You look at them and think, "Wouldn't you rather be somewhere else?"

In sports, this suspicion is often warranted. When your performance falters, it's probable your team *would* actually rather be with someone else.

That's why, in June 2003, I got a phone call that began, "Hi Ben, it's Dave Dombrowski."

Dave Dombrowski was general manager of the Detroit Tigers, a team that was on its way to having the worst season in American League history.

"I have good news, Ben," he said. "We got you in a trade today."

By Spring Training 2003, the massive quantities of medicine I'd been taking in order to stay on the field were starting to cause spastic movements, which is a common side effect of the drugs once they've been in your system awhile. On top of that, constant time-zone changes, day and night games, and an inconsistent diet made any sort of drug pattern — which is especially important to a Parkinson's patient — impossible to maintain.

My swing was funky, and at the plate I was making adjustments to my adjustments. I was constantly hooking the ball foul. Catching was a near impossibility, so I was now almost exclusively an outfielder. I noticed for the first time that I moved slower in real life than I did in my dreams.

The Rockies sent me to Triple-A Colorado Springs, with the prospect of returning to the big club highly uncertain. Something inside me started to swell — a seething combination of disappointment, regret and anger.

Illness is the most compressed of circumstances. Everything is in that collision. And as 2003 progressed, things inside me grew muddier and darker. The lit-from-within kid who danced with the Blues Brothers between innings dimmed to a flicker. I was disappearing.

When Dombroski called, he said the Tigers were offering me a chance to play in the big leagues for a coaching staff that included some of the stars from the Detroit team that won the 1984 World Series, including manager Alan Trammel and Lance Parrish.

But the name that got my attention was Kirk Gibson. As a player, Gibson was legendary for his fiery temperament, his uniform being constantly dirty, and the monumental home run he hit off Dennis Eckersley to win Game 1 of the 1988 World Series for the L.A. Dodgers.

I'd read his book, *Bottom of the Ninth*, at lightning speed. The chance to be close to Gibson made me a little more optimistic about the trade.

The Tigers were given my medical file and asked me about the "tremors" I'd reported in 2000. Fortunately I'd planned ahead and took a heavy dose of meds going into the physical. The pharmaceuticals coursing through my body created the illusion of normalcy, and I passed the exam without any trouble.

Less than 24 hours after joining the club, I was starting in left field at Chicago's Comiskey Park. There was one out and a runner at first base. Paul Konerko lined a ball into the leftfield gap. I raced over to it, pivoted and threw the ball on a perfect line to third. Shane Halter caught it and applied the tag, a split second after the lead runner reached the base.

Now, the correct play in that instance is to field the ball and throw it to second base, so as to hold the hitter at first and keep the double play in order. I should have thrown the ball to second, but got caught up in the chance to make a spectacular play. I was fortunate the hitter was Konerko, who's not the fastest guy, and he neglected to take second base despite my gaffe.

Between innings, Halter came up to me and said, "Great throw. Almost had him."

Gibson heard the comment, jumped up and absolutely shredded us. Using less polite words (most of which began with the letter "F") than I will here, he essentially said, "If you'd been playing good baseball you'd have thrown the ball to second."

I stayed in the big leagues for the rest of the season, popping pill after pill so I could remain in the lineup, all the while feeling less and less like myself. As a relatively new outfielder, I made some mistakes, with a red-faced Gibson drawing a bead on me every time. I always took his wrath, looking him in the eye, listening, and nodding as respectfully as I did to P.J. Carey eight years earlier when he told me to wear dress shirts to the yard. But each time Gibson got in my face, I felt a small part of the old me break away.

In mid-September, I was playing centerfield against the Indians. We had the lead late in the game, and I was playing deep with two outs so as not to allow any extra-base hits. There was a high pop up behind second base. I ran in as hard as I could, but my gate was uneven and the ball bounced violently in the high sky. Without a clear line on it, I pulled up, hoping our second baseman would make the play. The ball dropped between us. I was furious with myself for not getting to it. (Fortunately the next batter struck out and we won.)

After the game, I was in the training room icing my ankle. Sure enough, in walked Gibson.

"Gibby!" I shouted, putting my hand up. My body was vibrating like a tuning fork.

Startled, he came to a total stop.

"I don't want to hear it, Gibby!"

He nodded, turned and left the room, not saying a word.

I couldn't stop shaking.

I'd just yelled at Kirk Gibson. I'd just yelled at my coach.

I was officially a stranger in my body.

And though we shared a disease, I felt very little like my father's son.

RADIO SILENT

Sports are innocent, if for no other reason than its losses aren't real losses.

Maybe this explains my dad and the radio.

Though it wasn't said out loud, we all knew heading into the 2003 season that my career was winding down. This instinct was validated when I was dealt to the Tigers by the Rockies, who only 18 months before had told other general managers to not even bother bringing up my name in trade discussions.

My dad became possessed with the need to hear my games on the radio or via the Internet. Regardless of what was happening on a given day, he would exhaust every avenue possible to hear the broadcasts.

My brother called me after a party he'd attended with our folks, and told me that my dad had gone missing for awhile, only to be found sitting fixated by a computer in the host's office.

He did this for all 162 games that season, not so much listening as he was memorizing.

Sooner or later, we'd need to talk about things. For four years, we'd done this dance where we had the same diagnosis, but never discussed it. Both our careers were being torn asunder, but talking about that fact would have made it real.

Much like his son, my dad had soldiered on after his diagnosis, obstinately working as hard as ever. But he was clearly wearing down, so much so that his once powerful frame seemed to be deflating. That school year, a kid he was walking to the principal's office for disciplinary purposes simply ran away, and my dad could do nothing about it.

I imagine that "shame" can't begin to describe what he felt at that moment, nor can I imagine what it must have been like to relate that pain to your son, who was experiencing a magnified version of that shame daily in front of thousands.

Parkinson's comes with emotional issues that land heavily, even on its most tenacious sufferers: Embarrassment when holding up the line at the store while fumbling for your wallet. Self-consciousness as you watch your loved ones watch you, as you tread cautiously around a home now riddled with booby traps. Fear on top of fear that you'll slip irreversibly into dementia.

My dad was exceptional at keeping Parkinson's at a distance. "I have Parkinson's, but Parkinson's doesn't have me" became his go-to saying. But when your sole dream is to give your kid a better life than your own, only to see him overtaken by the same disease that has you in its grips … What must that be like?

Shakespeare wrote, "It is a wise father that knows his own child." Yet my dad may have been the only father alive who knew his boy *too* well.

He gave me wings, and now I was falling from a very, very high place. When something like this happens, you can do one of two things: 1) Be a coward and turn away; or 2) Do what great men do, and stand sentry for 162 games, never leaving your boy, no matter how twisted the pain.

Before I had my own family, if you asked me to explain who I was, I'd have brought up two things: sports and my father. The two were essentially interchangeable.

My dad's own father figures were coaches. It was through sports that he came to understand what it meant to be a man and to lead. So coach-speak became the fluency in our home, and sports the reason to talk, get together, argue, see the world and celebrate.

Even in less complicated times for our family, we sensed the eventual conclusion of our athletic careers might make for some awkward pauses with our dad. What would we talk about? Who would we be to one another?

Most kids have to balance a frightening sense your father is a god with the equal (and perhaps more frightening) possibility that he's just another man.

I always knew my dad was far more than just another man. But I did worry about him discovering that — in a world without sports — I was just another boy.

I saw my sister, Mari Lyn, work through similar concerns a year earlier. She'd been a standout softball player at Glencoe and got a scholarship to play at University of Oregon. She had a great freshman season, but got hurt during her sophomore year and lost her passion for the game. It was clear she wanted to shut it down.

Being that we're more than five years apart in age, Mari Lyn and I weren't terribly close at that point in our lives. But we found communion in her decision to put competitive sports aside. Like me, she was an anxious person, desperate to succeed and all too willing to relentlessly push herself to the outer boundaries of her ability. We were both motivated by fear, specifically the fear of disappointing our family by failing to extract every last reward our God-given ability might provide.

Mari Lyn and I had some long phone conversations, and I assured her it would be OK if she stopped playing. I found myself opening up to her, too, and I told her the truth about my life. She became my one indulgence — the keeper of my true identity.

The 2003 season came and went. The Tigers asked me to play winter baseball, and I refused because I didn't want to continue with the full-throttle overmedication that sustained me through the big-league season. The end of my career was just a formality at that point.

The night before I left for spring training in February 2004, I stopped by my parents' house. My sister was there and handed me a gift: two CDs she'd made, as well as a card. She explained that when I was under stress, I should listen to this music.

Turning to leave, I realized how profoundly I didn't want to walk out that door. I didn't want to leave because I knew I'd be coming back soon.

Mari Lyn walked up next to me. I softly put my head on her shoulders as she put her arms around me.

By mid-summer I was formally announcing my retirement, telling the world I had Parkinson's. My refusal to look the disease in the eye lasted until the end, as I insisted to the press the disease had not compromised my on-field performance.

I slunk back into Hillsboro, forever the man I used to be.

The next few years, a pursuit of magical medicines and alternative healers was my focus. Baseball clubhouses were replaced by doctors' waiting rooms. It was about as far from big-league glory as one could without a space rocket.

I often asked to bring my dad to these appointments, because doctors couldn't resist the incredibly rare chance to compare and contrast a father and son with a disease that supposedly had no genetic link.

We became something of a must-see act on the Parkinson's circuit. Even still, heart-to-heart conversations between my dad and I about our disease remained elusive.

One of these trips took me, Kellie and my dad back to Colorado. It proved to be yet another meeting filled at first with promise, only to end in crushing disappointment. We collapsed in the rental car, and drove in the dark along the same stretch of highway I'd taken the night I was called up to the majors, only this time heading the opposite direction.

We spent almost 90 minutes in total silence when my dad tried to kick up some small talk.

"It'll sure be nice when we figure this Parkinson's thing out and don't have to deal with it anymore," he said, smiling and doing his best to lift our spirits.

"Yeah," I murmured, keeping my eyes on the road.

"Then you guys can start a family," he said.

Kellie was sitting in the back seat, and we shared a knowing glance via the rear-view mirror. There was a long pause.

"I'm not sure that's going to happen," she said.

"Dad," I said, "with the seriousness of my health stuff, we're not sure it's a good idea to bring a child into this."

This brought us back to silence. My dad sat in the passenger seat, hands in his lap and looking down. A couple of times his head bobbed up like he was going to say something, but emotion stalled him.

Finally, the words jumped across the lump in his throat. After many years and hundreds of miles of highway, his thoughts came unchained.

"It's just not fair to you guys what's been happening," he said, tears streaming down his cheeks. "Being a father has been the greatest thing in my life. You two are good people, and for you not to have the same experience I've had would be a shame. Please don't give up. Please promise me you won't. Please ...

"For me to go through this is one thing, but not my son. Not my son. Please don't close the door on your family."

Two years later, Kellie and I would learn the parallel blessings of parenthood. You love your baby unconditionally, while hopefully in that same moment realizing you've been loved the same way your whole life by your own parents.

But in the car that night, Kellie and I could only sit in stunned silence.

Eventually, someone turned on the radio.

THE BICYCLE

In the film "The Tree of Life," the mother says in narration, "There are two ways through life — the way of nature and the way of grace. You have to choose which one you'll follow.

"Nature," she goes on to say, "only wants to please itself. Get others to please it, too. Likes to lord it over them. To have its own way. It finds reasons to be unhappy when all the world is shining around it.

"But grace doesn't try to please itself. Grace accepts being slighted, forgotten. Accepts insults and injuries."

It's not adequate to say that my mother possesses grace. Grace and my mother seemingly inhabit one another.

I'll pause right here to say I realize boys often write about their moms in awe-inspired terms, as if they're seeing the Grand Canyon for the first time. But if you met my mother, you'd know.

You'd know she's a revelation, like seeing *anything* for the first time must be.

How filled with grace is my mother? My father wet himself on their first date, and she still married him.

95

My dad was on football scholarship at Southern Oregon University, when into the cafeteria walked Marci Snyder, the shy daughter of a Methodist turkey farmer from Oregon City by way of Waverly, Neb.

"Gobble," he and his friends called out as she walked past. "Gobble, gobble, gobble."

I'm not sure how this technique brought down her defenses, but it did.

Their first date was to a dance. My dad arrived late with a big bandage around his knee, as he'd been injured in a game that day. At some point in the evening, the ice pack inside the bandage burst, soaking my dad's pants and bringing the night to an early conclusion.

He walked her home, and when they reached her dormitory, my dad asked his future wife three questions:

"Do you smoke?"

No.

"Do you drink?"

No.

"Do you believe in God?"

Yes.

With that, they were inseparable, and my dad had love in his life for the first time. My mom made him his first birthday cake. She brought him to church. She indulged his dream to become a coach, moving wherever and whenever. When they had children, she put her needs third, then fourth, then fifth without a trace of complaint — the personification of the Biblical saying, "Be joyful always. Give thanks in all circumstances."

Piano lessons. Paper routes. Games upon games upon games. Still, she found time to be a leader in our church, to work with emotionally disturbed kids, and cash in every coupon in a 10-mile radius.

Without exaggeration, the majority of my friends have never seen my mom sitting down unless she was in a car or a church.

Like anyone, she looked forward to the golden years of retirement and grandchildren. She talked with her sister about trips they'd take someday. She bought a bike, which she leaned up against the wall in the garage for future use.

Until that day came, every long trip would end up at a baseball diamond with a geometry identical to the last, which was fine with her so long as we were together.

The one time my mom was away from us for an extended period of time was when she drove back to Nebraska to take care of her grandfather, who had advanced-stage Parkinson's. He eventually died from its complications.

So when my dad's secretary said she'd noticed his hand trembling when he talked on the phone, my mom knew.

When he was announcing a volleyball game and couldn't hold the microphone steady, she knew.

And when her 22-year-old son reported he was having trouble with his left hand not doing what it was supposed to, and his feet were getting stiff … somewhere inside, she knew.

Doctors have said there is no genetic biomarker for Parkinson's. But if a disease can haunt a person, Parkinson's has haunted my mom.

My mom long ago earned the right to finally see the world. Yet she spends her precious years taking care of men who yearn only to be still.

Somehow she's endured these accidents of life without her smile leaving her face. Day after day, she goes from family member to family member, providing grace like a diver offering air from her tank.

No one does more for more.

They say the worst thing a person can experience in life is losing a child. I would think that somewhere close to that is seeing your boy watch himself slowly come undone, desperately grasping for normalcy when the opposite in clearly his fate. What must it be like to watch your kid turn into a one-armed guy, throwing punches at the wind?

But instead of looking away, my mother brought us closer.

Kellie and I had decided to follow my mom's lead and rely on grace. We decided to have a baby. The plan was that Kellie would teach, while I would stay home and take care of our kid. I told myself that I'd willed myself through four big-league seasons with Parkinson's. I could will myself to be a father.

One day, my mother called.

"The house across the street from ours is for sale," she said. "You should take a look."

Soon after, we were moving back to "Petrick Lane," across the street from my parents and two doors down from my brother. When we did, my mom surrendered any shred of independence she had left in favor of full-time grandmotherhood — all with a total absence of longing.

On days when I wasn't feeling too well — which became increasingly frequent as time passed — I'd bring our baby through my parents' garage and into their kitchen. My mother would take her in her arms, give me a knowing smile, put her hand on my shoulder, and walk me out.

Out of the corner of my eye, I'd catch a glimpse of her bike.

But she never did.

40,000 TO ONE

In 2003, I was traded to the Detroit Tigers, an extremely young team on its way toward finishing 47 games out of first place. Just three years later, they reached the World Series.

The very next year, my original team, the Colorado Rockies, made a miraculous run to the World Series behind Clint Hurdle and the group of players with whom I'd come up the ranks.

I wasn't there for either.

After my first game in the majors, *Baseball Daily* sent me a postcard that would be archived for posterity. They asked me to write down my memories of my first big-league hit, and any advice I might offer kids.

Already on the card was text that read, "On Wednesday, September 1, 1999, Ben Petrick made his much anticipated Major League debut at the age of 22. He fulfilled his boyhood dream of one day becoming a big league baseball player, which began the day he was born on April 7, 1977."

Underneath I wrote, "I can remember standing on second base after my first hit (an RBI double) and looking up at 40,000 fans giving a standing ovation."

Almost exactly eight years later, my audience had gone from 40,000 to one.

Typical guides for successful parenting don't include advice on overcoming rigidity that makes bending over impossible, dyskinesia that interferes with throwing, or garbled speech that makes it difficult to read a picture book at naptime. But we had faith, and on Sept. 7, 2007, Kellie and I became parents to Makena, a daughter named after the beach where we were married on Maui.

Our plan worried our loved ones, to say the least. Kellie would teach half time. I'd stay home and have primary childcare duties.

My rationale was this: Parkinson's had put me in some awkward spots. I'd spent my life straight and sober (with a few notable exceptions), and refused the lure of steroids even as my career slipped through my fingers. Now my entire world revolved around drugs.

I was raised to be an honorable person, yet I felt I had been forced to be less than truthful about my health with people and companies that had a stake in my physical performance.

I was a proud man, yet I'd sacrificed my reputation and allowed my name to become a metaphor for underachievement in baseball so I could play the game I loved (and make a living) just a little bit longer.

I had earned the deep friendship of some great people, yet was now closed off from most of them, feeling their valuable time was better spent with someone less tethered to a sad reality than I was.

I'd only wished for two things in life: to be a pro ballplayer and to be a father. Parkinson's took one of those. I wasn't going to let it have both.

The choice to take care of Makena alone came with the tradeoff that I'd have to endure some new physical challenges.

The first was exhaustion. I never got more than two or three hours of deep sleep a night, because Parkinson's never sleeps. When sufferers try to rest, the disease mounts a siege on our bodies. Most nights I was in bed by 9, and awake again by 1 or 2 a.m.. To be honest, I often didn't want to go to sleep, because Parkinson's inspires some crazy dreams that are often pretty terrifying. There'd be no opportunities to catch up on my rest, though, with a baby around.

The second physical challenge was hunger. I had to be available for Makena, which meant giving my medication every opportunity to work. Food only introduced variables, so I would eat early in the morning, and not again until right before bed. I did this despite the fact that I was constantly shaking from dyskinesia and therefore burning major calories. The hunger pangs could be surprisingly extreme.

A good day meant my meds worked as planned. This would occur maybe 75 percent of the time. After Kellie went to work around 10:30, Makena and I would play, have lunch, get her a nap, and read. We generally stayed very close to home, though, fearing a good medication day would turn bad without warning.

On days when my medication wasn't working, I'd hopefully be able to get Makena to my parents' house or pop in a movie to distract her. If that didn't happen, it could be intense, with her crying and needy, and me bound by invisible chains, unable to help. The best I could do was stumble around wearing a silly face, doing my best to distract and entertain.

When Makena was first born and these bad days were less frequent, my zest for life came back a little bit. After all, I was raising a child, doing the most important work in the world. Suddenly, I was more inclined to listen to the stories about someone's Uncle Bill who had Parkinson's for 40 years but died climbing Mt. Whitney at age 90. "That could be me," I'd think.

Unfortunately, my symptoms became much worse as Makena grew older. I was taking more and more medication to fight off rigidity, accepting ever-worsening spasticity as a consequence. Calls to my parents' house were becoming increasingly frequent.

Naturally, I was racked with worry that Makena was losing out because of my limitations. But sometimes I'd get a psychological break. Every so often, a ray of light would peek through that hinted this adventure of ours was helping her develop into a compassionate and charitable little girl.

By the time Makena turned 2, she had some sense that her dad once did something on TV that involved hitting and throwing a ball, even though we rarely talked about my past life.

She was just learning to speak. I was feeding her lunch, and for my own entertainment we were watching a story about Texas Rangers outfielder Josh Hamilton on TV.

Josh had been my teammate in the 2000 All-Star Futures Game. He was 19 and a year removed from going first in the draft to the Tampa Bay Devil Rays. I remember him being a really kind, quiet kid, not to mention a freakishly smooth athlete. Some scouts said he was the best prospect they'd ever seen.

But Josh fell prey to drugs and alcohol and was soon out of the game, only to resurrect his career in 2007.

Now Makena and I were watching a replay of Josh's legendary performance in the 2008 All-Star Home Run Derby at Yankee Stadium, where he hit 28 balls out in the first round. Each homer shook the stadium, like a dog playing with a rag.

The crowd started chanting, "Ham-il-ton! Ham-il-ton! Ham-il-ton!"

I looked away from the TV and over at Makena in her high chair, and gave her a little grin.

"Pretty cool, huh?" I asked. She just smiled.

I turned back toward the counter to finish making her lunch.

"Dad-dy!" Makena yelled out gleefully.

"Dad-dy! Dad-dy! Dad-dy!"

I wheeled around.

Makena looked toward the screen, smiling and pounding the base of her palms rhythmically. She stopped for a second and gave me a look that seemed to say, "It's OK, Dad. You're *my* home run hitter."

Then she picked up the beat again.

I only saw one pair of hands clapping. But I swore I heard 40,000.

"Dad-dy!"

"Dad-dy!"

"Dad-dy!"

TAKE THE WHEEL

I spent much of my post-baseball life surrounded by beautiful women, who because of me spent a good portion of their lives waiting in cars.

On one occasion, I was taking Makena, who was now 3, to swim lessons. But my medication hadn't worked as I thought it would, and as we pulled into the parking lot at the swim center, I went "off" and turned to stone.

"Let's go, Daddy," she said.

"Sweetie, I can't walk too good right now," I mumbled. "I need you to be patient, OK?"

At that moment, she could have screamed. She could have jumped out of the car and ran. She could have sold the car for parts. In any of these scenarios, I'd have been defenseless.

Instead she climbed into the front seat as she had too many times before, looked at me with too-understanding eyes, and said, "OK, Daddy." Then she kissed my cheek, put her head on my shoulder, and waited.

She learned this move from her mom.

I was less than a year from making my big-league debut when I met Kellie Starkey at a Halloween party on the Oregon State campus. She was four years younger than I was, but I was captivated. It was one of those rare moments in life where you don't need the benefit of hindsight to know the importance of what's happening before your eyes.

Kellie was a force. She seemed to contain all ages and all seasons — worldly without actually having seen the world; wise without having to age. I knew two things right away: First, that her life would be utterly without boundaries; and second, that I wanted to see that life take place.

We dated for five years, and Kellie was my peaceful refuge despite much of our relationship taking place long distance. Whenever she'd come to visit, it felt like my world would go from black and white to color.

I loved her tenacity. She had the same drive academically that I had in sports, getting a 4.0 all the way through school. But what I came to love most about Kellie was that she was both great and good. For all of her accomplishments, she was even better on the inside. She was exceptionally pretty, but her essential goodness had a hold on me even more than her beauty. I knew I could stake my life on her friendship a thousand times and she'd never fail me.

As my health picture came into focus, it became more and more evident that I wasn't just in love with any woman, but *exactly* the right woman. Only the determined and independent Kellie Starkey could say, "I can do this," and have me believe her. In an odd way, the obstacle of my disease made it even more apparent we should be together.

We were married not long after I retired. For our honeymoon we took a cruise to Alaska. We were sitting on our balcony, and I'd just defeated Kellie in Scrabble for the first time ever when a pod of humpback whales started breaching right before our eyes.

We're going to be OK, I thought.

Maybe even better than OK.

Flash forward a decade, and countless times this woman in the prime of her life had been forced to be my caretaker. I did all I could to keep the burden from her, but there were times when I was so overcome that the need for her to act as my nurse couldn't be avoided.

In just a handful of years, I'd gone from a somebody to a sideshow — a one-time physical specimen who now needed his wife's help tying his shoes. Evenings that should have been spent out and about ended instead with my young wife helping her weary, stilted husband change into his nightclothes. Night after night, I was Pinocchio in reverse, turning from man to wood.

Now I was relegated to a life fueled by regret for having taken Kellie and Makena captive. Worse yet, I sensed the sadness that was like steam in my veins was now fogging Kellie's life, too. In my mind, she was stuck in an existence no one would want, watching everything she had a right to expect from life get deconstructed, day by cloistered day. Sometimes I'd feel more immobilized by worry for her than by Parkinson's.

After awhile, whenever Kellie entered my field of vision, the same two words would race to my lips:

"I'm sorry."

At the top of the list of things I felt I'd stolen from my wife's life was spontaneity. I'm not talking about "grab your passport" spontaneity, either. I'm talking "let's go to a movie" spontaneity. Countless attempts to do anything outside the Parkinson's regimen resulted in failures to launch, with us sitting frustrated in a parking lot, waiting for me to go from "off" to "on."

I first became aware of Deep Brain Stimulation (DBS) surgery in 2003 when I was playing for the Tigers. I turned on the television in my hotel room and watched a news program about how Parkinson's patients were undergoing a radical treatment involving the implantation of electrodes within the brain. Electrical impulses transmitted from a battery implanted in the chest to the electrodes had the effect of lessening Parkinson's symptoms and decreasing the need for medication in some patients. That all sounded good, but the surgery was disturbing (with the patient awake for much of it), risky and terrifying to contemplate.

"If I ever get to a point where I'm even considering something that gross, I'm done," I thought to myself.

But by 2009, I was desperate. I had to do something to drastically alter the path my wife and child were having to travel with me.

Ten years earlier, I was told about a cyclist named Davis Phinney, who also lived in Colorado and was diagnosed with young-onset Parkinson's at the age of 40. I did nothing with that information, but in mid-2009 I heard somewhere that Davis had undergone DBS, with amazing results.

Davis, who was an Olympic medalist and the first American to win a Tour de France stage, was now reclaiming his life after a shaken decade — in fact, he was off Parkinson's medication entirely.

Davis and I began speaking by phone, and he told me there were now times when he forgot he even had the disease.

"Think about your wife and daughter," said Davis, trying to elicit in me the courage I was having difficulty mustering on my own. "Think about how a successful surgery would affect them."

It worked.

After one too many times not being able to pick up Makena when she needed me, I decided to pursue DBS.

I underwent some preliminary exams that November at Stanford Medical Center in Palo Alto, Calif., and was scheduled for surgery on Dec. 18, 2009, a Thursday. I'd need to be in town by Tuesday for some tests. As luck would have it, the San Francisco 49ers (my favorite team) were playing just up the road from Stanford against the Arizona Cardinals that Monday night.

Kellie is every bit the sports fan I am — a three-sport athlete in high school and a devoted tailgater at Oregon Ducks football games since the age of two. One of her fondest childhood memories is of her eighth-grade year when Glencoe High won the 1995 state football championship — my team.

In a burst of spontaneity I hoped would signal things to come for Kellie and me, I pulled some strings and got two tickets to see the Niners.

Unfortunately, that excitement quickly gave way to a serious sense of foreboding in the weeks leading up to the surgery. The procedure seemed like a combination of medieval medicine and science fiction. I kept asking myself, "Is this the sort of risk a family man should take?"

The answer kept coming back the same: "This is *exactly* the sort of risk a family man should take." If I made it through, our lives would be better. If I didn't, *their* lives would still be better.

Before we left for California, I made videos for my family. My tone was that of a guy whose bags were packed, and who was truly, deeply sorry to be leaving.

I told my parents how thankful I was to have been raised by them. I told them that, in case it was on their minds, I didn't blame them for my getting Parkinson's.

I told my brother and sister how much I appreciated their support throughout my life, and especially when I became a disabled father. I asked that they always find time for Makena so she would have some sense of who I was as a person.

I told Makena how sorry I was to have put this on her, but I needed her to be a big girl and take care of Mommy. I told her I did this so that we could have a simpler life together. Obviously, if she was watching this video, it meant God had other plans for our family. I told her to be a positive person and let her light shine on as many people as possible — to be a good influence on society and never one who drags it down. I told her that she might someday — if not already — have another daddy in her life, and that she should support him, treat him like her real daddy and be a good girl.

I told her she was the best thing that ever happened to me.

After a day of travel, Kellie and I arrived in San Francisco and headed to the game early, wanting to be there in plenty of time to watch warm-ups. I took my medication right on schedule … and nothing happened.

In a few days, I would be undergoing a surgery I once considered unthinkable, with potentially fatal consequences.

These might be my last days with my wife. It didn't seem like a lot to ask that we be able to watch the Niners get loose. But there we sat in the rental car, with the crowd shuffling past as we waited for my meds to kick in. After an hour and a half, I took another dose. Darkness fell, and we listened to the start of the game on the radio.

There I was with a beautiful woman, waiting in a car — again.

Three days later, Kellie would push me through the Stanford Medical Center doors in a wheelchair. I took solace that no matter what, it would be my last slice of humble pie.

Back home, a video waited for Kellie, too.

I told her that I knew our life together had gotten tedious. I knew there was no spontaneity. I didn't want her to spend the rest of her life having to think about bringing medication, making sure we had enough, knowing when to take it, watching what I ate — all to have a trace amount of normalcy.

I told her I knew I was a far cry from the person she fell in love with. She deserved more than the husk of a man I'd become.

I told her that it was OK if she chose to marry someone else to help her raise Makena.

"Please just make sure he deserves the two of you," I said. "Please make sure he's a good guy.

"And, Kellie … I love you, Kellie. I'll be so sad if I don't have the chance to grow old with you. But no matter what happens, the decision we made to have this surgery was the right one. Never doubt that."

I told her that whether I lived or died, at least there'd be no more waiting.

A FAVOR TO ASK

Who are you?" I asked, waking up from my nap.

The boy on the other side of my bedroom looked to be maybe 8 or 9 — about my age. He was smaller than I was, and had a riot of blonde, curly hair. He stared at the floor.

"Erik," he said quietly. "I just moved in next door."

"Why are you playing with my toys?" I asked.

"Sorry," he said, putting them down. "Your mom let me in."

In a childhood filled with good fortune, perhaps none was better than the day Erik Aartsen moved into the house behind ours.

On the surface, we were opposites back then. I was in perpetual motion, while Erik could barely do anything physical without breaking a wrist or knocking himself unconscious. If there was an upturned rake on which to step, Erik would miraculously find it.

But Erik had an incredible mind. We had one of the original Macintosh computers, which my dad had secured through some teacher connection or other. He installed a flight simulator game, which had to be controlled with keystrokes. I could stand to play the thing for about 45 seconds before crashing and running outside. One day I came downstairs, and Erik was playing on the simulator, flying underneath the Golden Gate Bridge.

Soon we found common ground — and by common ground I mean we both put on football pads, bounced as high as we could on a trampoline, and tried to create the craziest mid-air collisions possible.

More than 25 years later, we were husbands and fathers. We were still best friends. And on one particular night, we sat together at the edge of the world.

A few weeks earlier, I was wheeled on a gurney into Deep Brain Stimulation surgery at Stanford Medical Center, and my last thoughts before I went under were, "I can't believe I have to do this."

Then darkness.

I resurfaced to a voice saying, "Mr. Petrick, you are waking up in the operating room."

Doctors had drilled two holes in my skull, and they were now exploring the middle of my brain trying to find the *substansia nigra* so they could implant a tiny device. The brain doesn't have any nerve endings, so I couldn't feel a thing.

A movement-disorder specialist stood at the foot of my bed, smiling. I hadn't taken any medication going into surgery, so my body had receded to its natural, Parkinson's-induced state, meaning I was totally cramped, flexed and shaken. A massage therapist worked on my legs and feet, trying to make me as comfortable as possible.

One doctor had on headphones, which were hooked into a computer that listened to the neurons in my brain firing. She moved my wrists, hands, elbows, legs and ankles. (When the brain tells a part of the body to move, it produces the electrical sounds she was tracking.)

The lead neurosurgeon called out signals like a quarterback, letting everyone know where he was in the brain. Then he found the right spot.

"Mr. Petrick," he said, "we're going to give you a little preview of what life will be like when your procedures are complete."

The doctor with the earphones turned on the electric stimulation and for an instant I felt a little buzz down half my body.

"Ben, try to move your hand like you're screwing in a lightbulb," she said. They'd asked me to do the same thing going into the surgery, and I couldn't. But now I could make the motion without any trouble at all.

I started laughing. For a blessed few seconds, I remembered my old body.

"*There* you are," I thought.

They repeated the process on the other side.

More laughing.

"Mr. Petrick," the neurosurgeon said, "you've done very well. We had a good day today. We're going to put you back to sleep and you'll wake up in the recovery room."

Then darkness.

The doctor told my parents and Kellie it couldn't have gone better. A CAT scan the next day confirmed that everything was perfectly in order.

There were still two procedures to go. In three days, the doctors would attach wires to the electrodes that had been implanted in the first surgery, then run those wires under my forehead and down my neck, connecting them to a battery implanted in my chest that functioned like a pacemaker. Two weeks after that, the whole system would be turned on.

The wiring procedure went as perfectly as the first, according to my doctor.

"Now we just have to be patient," he told my family. "We want all the swelling to go down and for the brain to be as healed as possible before we flip the switch and activate everything."

They were allowing me to return to Hillsboro for Christmas as I awaited my third and final procedure. I was tired and sore, but otherwise optimistic. When we returned home, Makena came up to me and made a sad face.

"Oh," she said, "Daddy has an owy." She kissed my scalp and hugged me.

I can't imagine there's been a sweeter feeling in the history of man's existence.

A few days passed, and I was still having cognitive problems. I couldn't remember basic names or words, or passwords on the computer. The doctors assured us this was normal.

Seven days after surgery — Christmas Day — I was still exhausted, and spent most of the day napping in my chair. I had no appetite.

Two days after that, I was sitting in our living room when out of the corner of my eye I saw a blue jay land on our window ledge. This triggered the first of what would be numerous seizures. My head was like a sprinkler — I couldn't stop it from pivoting left, then right. This went away, then resumed an hour later. We called the nurse advisor, who said to get to the emergency room immediately.

The events that followed are a gauzy, semi-conscious blur.

I remember waking to find my father in law standing beside my bed, and apologizing to him over and over for putting his daughter through this. "She deserves better," I told him. "She doesn't deserve this. I'm so sorry."

The seizures grew in severity. A brain scan revealed I had a massive infection in the surgical area. The whole apparatus would need to be removed. Have the operation or die, they said.

The electrodes were removed, and a catheter was inserted into my chest so antibiotics could go straight to my heart and be dispersed immediately throughout my body.

Soon, though, it felt like there was a switchblade in my skull and it was trying to burrow its way to daylight. The doctors prescribed meds, but nothing could touch the shrieking pain. I held my head and screamed.

The nurses asked if I wanted morphine.

"Yes!" I begged. "Just fast! Please! Fast!"

A nurse quickly shot morphine into the catheter.

Just as she began to say, "This might cause nausea," I vomited, and continued to for the rest of the night.

I had another MRI, and the infectious disease doctor determined an abscess had formed around one of the electrode sites. "We can either treat it with more antibiotics," he said, "or we could do another surgery to drain the abscess and inject antibiotics directly into the site."

I had surgery again. It was my fourth brain surgery in two weeks.

The doctors told my folks that everything had gone as well as they could have hoped. Now it was just a matter of letting the antibiotics kill the bacteria that had infected my brain. We could only wait, and they cautioned the next few days might not be pleasant.

The next week was an inferno. I was unable to get my Parkinson's meds to work for more than an hour, and the disease roared through my body with abandon.

For so long I'd coexisted with the disease; made peace with its deception. If my disease had a sound, it was, as John Irving wrote, "a sound like something trying not to make a sound." Each day, Parkinson's and I did our little dance, with me taking medicine, and the disease trying to sneak around it. For years, the best it could do was sneak in a side door.

But now, with no one guarding my house and the front door open, Parkinson's was inhabiting me fully.

I was drenched in sweat and drowning in exhaustion, with each day growing more agonizing as the disease ran roughshod, taunting and mocking my inability to stop it.

On Day 1, I leaned on a walker to get to the bathroom, but by Day 3 it was useless. By that third day, I couldn't feed myself, couldn't go to the bathroom by myself, couldn't hold a glass of water by myself. My wife fed and bathed me like an invalid. I thought I was going to be paralyzed for the rest of my days.

Now I just wanted out, out, out.

I wanted to end it right then, to rescue my wife and my child from the tempest of my existence — and to free myself from the relentless *bam-bam-bam* of ferocious guilt that thundered in me.

On the fourth night, Erik came to relieve my family. I'd never allowed myself to be seen in anywhere near as vulnerable a state as this. But there I was, the former brawn to Erik's brain, now unable to feed myself.

Ten years before, when I was given my diagnosis of "Parkinsonism," I allowed myself 60 seconds of emotion. For the next decade, I refused to speak of my illness, let alone indulge it with tears. I would not dignify Parkinson's with my feelings. It had stolen my career, my money, my body, my father's body, and my parents' golden years.

But it would not steal my toughness.

I would not even say its name. I would let them say that I couldn't handle the pressure of big-league ball. I would let them say the responsibilities of catching were too much — heck, I'd say it myself if it would distract them from the truth. I would defy my moral code and not be forthright about what was happening to me.

And until the day I retired, I would not say my disease's name. Even after that, I would not let it make me cry. I would not distinguish this cowardly illness that would embezzle everything but my mind, leaving me fully conscious of my own demise.

Yet there I was, flayed open with a fire coursing though me. I hadn't slept in three days. My body was completely flexed and shaking intolerably. I could not get remotely comfortable. Occasionally I would somehow come to a standing position on the bed — a man possessed. Erik was doing all he could, massaging my feet, trying to get the dystonia out. Lightning scissored through my body, and it felt for all the world like Erik, who'd been there at the dawn of my life, would also be there for its dusk.

Then it happened.

Tears began to flow from my eyes, and then Erik's.

Every microbe of my physical being wanted to fling myself into the abyss. I was alive with death.

But up from the deepest bay of my mind, a tiny voice kept surfacing:

You can.

For hours, that small voice beat back the flames that wanted to reduce me to nothing more than a pile of sobs and hate and shame, then steal the wind from me altogether. Oblivion welled and swelled inside me, but again and again that small voice fought it for the right to my life.

You can, she said.

So I growled. I foamed. I raged with a fury I never would have thought could exist within the walls of a man.

"I just want to be a regular dad for her, Erik!" I cried.

"I know, Ben," he replied, working feverishly to give me an comfort despite the obvious futility of his efforts.

"I want to see our kids grow up together, man! I just want to hear them laugh ..."

"I know."

Now I was sobbing. We both were.

"I just want to see my baby again! I just want to be her dad!" I growled.

I've always been a Christian and a believer, though I'd kept that part of my life mostly under wraps, even from Erik. To do otherwise required a level of security I never had. But the last vestiges of my every excess emotion were set aflame and consumed that night.

"Erik, I have a favor to ask."

"Anything," he replied.

I pried my hand from the bedrail and reached toward him.

"Pray with me."

BACK TO THE BOAT

My entire life, I'd played the little brother role. For this reason, I have my real older brother, and several honorary ones. Each of them had a similar disposition about my disease on the rare occasions I'd allow them to see me.

It was a deep-down feeling of sadness over the fact they couldn't protect me. When they'd see me coming toward them, bobbing and shuffling, they'd all take on the same wounded expression, as if they'd somehow failed me.

A few years after I'd retired, the FOX Network was developing a program called "Legacy," which put a reality TV spin on the classic movie "It's A Wonderful Life." Each week, they would surprise a person who'd gone through a life-altering circumstance, and walk them back through their younger days, showing them the impact they'd had on the world.

I was somehow chosen as the subject for the show's pilot. I was led to believe we were filming a show about my brother and his standout career as a teacher and coach. But when we all gathered, the veils were pulled up and I was told the show would be about me.

In the eyes of many, I'd just disappeared from baseball (and life), and the hope was this would bring me some happiness and peace.

My brother and I were whisked all around the country on a private plane, and our last stop was Denver. Coors Field, the Rockies home park, was lit up and entirely empty except for the two of us. We were led to the clubhouse, where we were surprised by a bunch of my old teammates and Rockies staffers.

We popped some beers. The guys faced me and told me things they didn't get a chance to when I abruptly left the game. They said they cared for me, that we'd always be teammates, and whether I felt it or not, they were always there if I needed them.

My brother was seated behind me as we filmed this, and what I couldn't see until I viewed the edited version of the show is that he was crying, something I'd rarely seen him do, if ever.

And he's crying *hard*. It all came to a head: the realization he couldn't protect me, and neither could any of these guys. I was an underdog in a fight with no "overdog." No matter what, the cells in my brain were dying, and a billion big brothers couldn't change that. The game was rigged.

Brotherhood could only take me so far. They couldn't take on this bully. It was something I ultimately had to do alone.

And I did.

Eight months after my DBS surgery, I attended an event called "Shake It Till We Make It," hosted by Brian Grant, the former NBA power forward who was diagnosed with young-onset Parkinson's at the age of 39. Brian lived in Portland and we'd become friends.

Brian had been a power forward's power forward: a beast on the boards; a double-double machine; an enforcer in the paint; and a quiet dirty-work guy happy to deflect attention to others. He was one of those classic "Give Me Five" guys, in that you could just hear a basketball coach saying "Give me five Brian Grants, and no one will have a chance against us."

After 12 NBA seasons, Brian retired in 2007 due to a bone-on-bone condition in his knee. At the time, he was just beginning to feel a slight tremor in his fingers. He tried to ignore it, and booked job interviews with TNT and CNN, where he'd hoped to sign on as a broadcaster. But the tremor got worse, and he didn't show for the interviews. He said, "I missed a lot of things because I didn't want people to look at me like I was weak; like 'something is wrong with me.' I didn't want people to think, 'He's broken.'"

After going through a really dark period, Brian started laying the groundwork for a foundation to raise awareness around Parkinson's. "Shake It Till We Make It" came soon after, attended by our fellow Parkinson's sufferers Michael J. Fox and Muhammad Ali, as well as superstars like Bill Walton, Charles Barkley and Bill Russell.

As Michael told Brian at the event, "With this disease, you don't pray for a lighter load; you pray for broader shoulders. And you have the broadest shoulders I've ever seen."

The keynote speaker at the event was Brian's former coach in Miami, Pat Riley. Riley coached four Lakers teams to NBA championships, and won another in 2006 with the Heat after sending Brian to L.A. in a package that brought back Shaquille O'Neal.

That night, Riley called Brian one of his "Forever Guys."

Forever Guys were players with "warrior" spirits Riley had coached along the way in Los Angeles, New York and Miami. He gave these guys "Forever" cards, signifying that no matter where and when, Riley would be there for them if they needed him. He promised his Forever Guys that he would be strong for them when they couldn't be strong for themselves.

But when Riley spoke that evening, he echoed the emotion my brother felt that night a few years earlier in the clubhouse at Coors Field:

You can be there. You can be strong. But you can't save. If there's saving to be done, it has to be done alone.

Riley said he'd cried three times in his career. The first was when Magic Johnson told him he'd contracted HIV. The second was when Alonzo Mourning told him he had a severe kidney ailment. The third was when Brian called and said he had Parkinson's.

Riley cried, he said, because a million Forever cards couldn't fix the problem. No one could save these men but themselves. Fortunately, Riley said, "I knew those three would 'swim back to the boat.'"

Then Riley told a story about a time he went whitewater rafting, and the guide told the group that if you fell out of the boat and into the rapids, you would be alone for a while — the boat couldn't stop for you. You'd have to take part in your own survival. Getting back to the boat was up to you.

Riley said that getting a devastating diagnosis was like falling out of the boat. You could simply get caught up in the rapids and watch the boat get smaller as it floated away, or you could fight your way back to it.

Stuck in these rapids, man would find his essential self, stripped bare of all else. The common man would just drift. Fortunately, Riley said, Magic, 'Zo and Brian fought as he knew they would. They fought their way back to the boat. They're all uncommon men, he said.

I'd been special my entire life. But I had no idea if I was uncommon.

I found the answer when I was in that hospital room for 12 ghastly days after my Deep Brain Stimulation surgery had gone so horribly wrong. Unable to feed or even relieve myself without help, I had every justification to end it all —

if not for myself, then for those innocent parties caught up in my life.

But then I thought about my daughter, at home having breakfast without me. I wanted so much to sit there with her, run my hand through those blonde curls, look into those blue eyes and listen to her say anything at all.

So I fought. The surgery didn't work the way we'd wanted, and I was physically worse off for having done it. But I was alive, and driving home from the hospital after those 12 days, I felt as fortunate as any man alive. In a few more miles, the car would pull down our oak-covered lane, I'd go inside, and I'd get to sit down for breakfast. I'd look into those blue eyes again and listen to my girl say anything at all.

And that's what I did. Watching Makena eat her breakfast, I realized I didn't lose my mind because of who I was carrying in my heart.

I knew going into it that parenting was the most vital job in the world, and it would require all I had to give. But how could I have known that my baby would be more important to me than I was to her? Her love was a net, and it caught me.

I don't know why I did it, but in that desperate hour I allowed myself to feel one last compliment. I allowed myself to feel that someone needed me.

So I fought my way back to the boat. I was proudly, certifiably uncommon. I'm not sure I was extraordinary at any point prior, but in what is the darkest hour for most people, I was at my best.

As a result, I was no longer just my parents' son, nor just Hillsboro's native son, a guy with a gift, or a guy with a disease. I was more than the sum of things I had nothing to do with. My life was finally mine.

I took satisfaction in this as Riley continued to speak.

But I couldn't get my mind off the Forever cards.

When we get married and have children, we give our wife and kids a Forever card. It signifies that we'll be there for them yesterday, today and always..

My life had been utter pandemonium. In that darkest hour, though, the answer to what I should do next became clear. I put the needs of those I loved ahead of my own. I made the simple decision to serve their needs, and took my own out of the equation. From there, the choice to fight wasn't a choice at all. It was a fact.

This is what I learned in the hospital: It's not about who's in the water. It's about who's in the boat.

I also thought about that moment on the operating table; that little window where my body felt "on" without the medication. In that moment, life rushed through me again.

That bell couldn't be un-rung. Now I knew there was another way for me to feel. There could be another, better life for Kellie and Makena — a life that included me.

Going back in for another try at DBS was terrifying and unfathomable on the surface. Then again, knowing what I knew, what good were the Forever cards I'd given my girls if I didn't go back?

I'd fought my way back to the boat. Sitting safely in it once again, I decided to do the uncommon:

I jumped back in the water.

GET ON THE BUS

I'm 34 years old.

It's Spring 2011, and I've had Parkinson's for 12 years.

I'm on a yellow school bus with 15 teenage boys on a 40-mile drive from Hillsboro to Tigard, Ore.

The bus is cold. The seats are hard. The music is unlistenable. Something smells.

I'm wearing exceptionally tight pants.

I'm happy.

"Hey, bro," I say, getting the attention of my buddy from high school, Markus Glaze, who is now the varsity pitching coach at Glencoe. "I really missed this."

What I remember about riding the bus in the minors is that it wasn't all that bad. You hear crazy stories, but I sort of liked it — the Latin players in the back blaring their merengue; getting taken to school playing Spades; learning "Baseball Spanish" (curse words only). Even when I didn't love it, I certainly didn't mind it.

I remember in Double-A, when I was playing for the Carolina Mudcats, we had a night game in Orlando, after which we were supposed to drive 12 hours back home for a game the next day. As I boarded the bus, I asked the driver jokingly, "Did you get a good nap in, Bussy?"

"No," he answered stone-faced. "Why?"

I laughed. "You do know that we're driving all the way back home tonight, right?" I asked.

"Seriously?" he replied.

Uh-oh, I thought. This is *not* good.

We took off and eventually everyone fell asleep. I woke up, and gazed out the windshield at the dark thickets of spruce trees on either side of us, as well as the dotted line splitting the highway.

Then I noticed us drifting over that line, before correcting quickly back.

I got up and quickly walked down the aisle between the seats of snoozing players, stepping over legs and heads that were lying across the aisle. Finally, I reached the driver.

"Bussy," I said quietly so as not to wake anyone. I got no response, so I said it again with a bit more volume. "BUSSY! How you doin' up here?"

He looked back with dark eyes. "I'm hurtin'," he said.

I quickly woke some older guys up to get their input on the situation.

Our first thought was, "Who else can drive this bus?" The answer: nobody.

Our second thought was, "What do we have in our bags to wake Bussy up?"

Out came the Mountain Dew and the caffeine pills. Pretty soon we couldn't shut Bussy up, so much so that we took turns sitting with him so the others could sleep. We pulled safely into our destination at 9 a.m., caught some shuteye, and played that night in a cotton-like humidity in front our own fans and some massive local bugs.

Making the transition from the busses I rode in the pros to the yellow bus I was on now had been more trying than I'd expected.

When my Parkinson's became insurmountable and I had to retire, I told myself the game just wasn't fun anymore. Baseball had run its course, and now I could move on.

I would do what I'd always planned: go back home, get my college degree, and do some coaching. I'd also be a spokesman for Parkinson's research and take advantage of the platform I was given. I'd be a good example to others. Sufferers everywhere would come to believe Superman wore Ben Petrick pajamas. I'd be inspiration exemplified.

But I didn't have the stuff to be a hero. That was the truth. I just wanted to go inside. If I couldn't be seen as strong, I didn't want to be seen.

On the field, I had been relentless and overpowering. I was stronger, faster and more willful than anyone out there. Fate was so strong in me that sometimes it felt like it had it's own breath.

Never in a million years did I think I could be as *human* as Parkinson's made me feel.

The frailty of genius is it needs an audience. Without my gift, I was desperately lonely. I moved home to a place where they'd once chanted my name, but from my disposition you'd have sworn I was new in town.

My mother tells a story about how soon after I was born, a friend of hers returned from a trip abroad with water from the Jordan River. My parents used that water to baptize me. I suppose that was the start of my preparing for something big. Wherever we went, ladies would say, "Well look at YOU! Aren't you CUTE?" In third grade, I'd practice signing autographs, including my uniform number.

I remember the way that made me feel. Even then I was so scared that feeling would go away. Appearing special eventually became more important to me than being special.

So instead of doing as I should have — instead of using my unique voice to raise awareness for this disease, and instead of being a leader of young men — I hid. I cowered. I made it clear I had little desire to make or sustain connections with anyone.

Things got worse for me physically. I constantly inhabited one of two bodies: Statue Ben, the natural state my body sought; and Bobbing-and-Weaving Ben, where I was freed from rigidity to the opposite extreme, with my medication inducing uncontrollable movements. My speech ranged from a rumble at worst to a grumble at best, and in all cases virtually unintelligible. The Devil's deal I'd made in massively over-medicating so I could keep playing baseball had come due. Now both Parkinson's personas lived in my one skin.

This was more reason to stay in the house. And yet being in our home, with my wife and daughter, was also torturous at times. They were so close, yet felt so far away. The thought, "I am less than you deserve" reverberated constantly in my head.

I could make peace with the fact I was not the man I thought I'd become. But this person — locked inside and governed by fear — was unacceptable. Intolerable. Something had to be done, which is why I chose to go ahead with Deep Brain Stimulation despite the risks.

My first attempt at DBS went very wrong, and nearly killed me. But I went back. Almost one year to the day after having the first surgery, I went in again, this time at Oregon Health & Science University (OHSU).

It worked.

For the first time in years, I could sit peacefully and calmly. I could walk to the kitchen to get breakfast in the morning and eat dinner at night with my family. I could play with my daughter, whenever she asked. I could help. I could sleep.

Going in for surgery again was both scary to the power of a million, and not scary at all. Winston Churchill said, "If you find yourself in hell, keep going." There's something liberating about having experienced the tortures of the damned and lived.

Things were just clearer this time around. Once I had control of my mind, wisdom seemed to follow naturally. My whole life, I worried about not being perceived as perfect.

Parkinson's burned down that house, and then some. It took me to a place where I didn't care about anything I didn't need. It took away every excess and need for absolute certainty.

All that remained was a guy who believed in something larger than himself, and a lover of those who put their heads down under the same roof as him each night. Period. That's all.

I didn't have surgery so I could go back to who I was. I did it so I could become the best version of whoever I was to be.

The second surgery did not make me perfect. I still tremor. I still go "off" and I still need medication. The magnitude of all of these is greatly lessened, though. The surgery allowed me to build a bridge back to those I loved, letting me do the little things I craved. It also built a bridge back to baseball.

Not long after I had retired, on a rainy afternoon, I was ushered to the high school. There was a surprise ceremony waiting, and they christened the Glencoe baseball diamond as "Ben Petrick Field."

A couple years later, I bumped into someone I used to know from Hillsboro who acted as if he'd seen a ghost.

"Geez, Ben," he said. "We haven't seen you for so long, and when they named that field after you, I thought you'd died."

Now Ben Petrick was back, coaching baseball on Ben Petrick Field — and loving the bus rides when we played on the road, even with the cold, the smell, the music and the tight pants.

An hour before I left to meet the yellow bus that day, I pulled on a baseball jersey for the first time in ages, and smiled at how it didn't fit me like it used to.

"Daddy," Makena asked, "are you playing baseball again?"

This question would have crushed me in the past, but no longer. Now life was about Makena, her mom, and the person I was becoming.

"Nah," I replied. "Just going to help some big kids and watch them play."

Each day I get a little stronger about being weaker.

NIGHT BECOMES US

My 4-year-old daughter's voice woke me up at 2:30 recently. It was a moment I'd been waiting for since the day she was born ...

At night I don't take any medication for my Parkinson's disease, because in the long run it makes my symptoms worse.

Pre-surgery, this was my routine:

 Bedtime typically came around 9:30, with me dressed in a sleek workout shirt and shorts. For Parkinson's patients, our sleeping hours require as much careful negotiation as our waking ones, and something as seemingly unthreatening as a blanket can become a sarcophagus. I wore the silky clothes to eliminate as much friction as possible.

The night usually began pretty innocently. The medication that kept my body limber during the day was typically still working when I climbed in bed, and I'd fall asleep within seconds of closing my eyes.

Days spent in perpetual movement, followed by claustrophobic nights where I could not move at all, created a level of insane exhaustion. Before surgery, I went about four years without so much as one recuperative night's sleep. This is something they never tell you about chronic illness — that you can get to the point where you feel like you might collapse under your own fatigue.

I'd sleep heavily for 2-3 hours, and then the dynamic part of my night would begin. By that point my medication would have completely worn off, with dystonia setting in as I laid there rigid as a plank, save for my arms shaking by my sides. In super-slow motion, I'd reach for an anti-anxiety pill on my nightstand, which I'd discovered through trial and error could sometimes relax me and my cramping muscles enough to get back to sleep.

Occasionally I'd get back to sleep, but most of the time self-loathing would take its place. My mind would take a tour of the scenarios in which I'd be totally helpless: robber, earthquake, alien abduction ...

Sleep or no sleep, I was fully awake by 3 or 4 a.m. If I had to relieve myself, I'd roll/fall out of bed and crawl to the bathroom. My toddler could walk herself to the bathroom, but I had to crawl.

My brain was now fully turned on, with Parkinson's following like a tail on a kite. Within minutes, dystonia would curl my bare feet into little fists. Michael J. Fox taught me a trick to deal with this: put on your patent-leather dress shoes to make your feet lie flat.

With that 10-minute task accomplished, my next destination was my recliner chair, a mere 100 feet and one treacherous stairwell away.

Once down the steps, I'd pass by my office full of baseball memorabilia, including a sign that once hung in the Rockies weight room that reads, "The vision of a champion is someone who is bent over, drenched in sweat, at the point of exhaustion, when nobody else is watching." Yet there I stood with no one watching, feeling distinctly unlike a champion.

I'd fall like a cut-down tree into the recliner, inch my finger toward the remote control, and search for a distraction until 6 a.m. Sitting in the new day's gloaming, I could finally take my medicine, then feel it warm the toes of my left foot like the sun rising over a basin. I craved that sensation — I was an addict, for sure. Dyskinesia would soon follow, sending my hands flailing and my head rolling. Before long I'd be negotiating the unique challenges of a Parkinson's sufferer, including buttoning my shirt, pouring milk, and holding the phone.

But for those first few minutes when my two little pills would take hold, it was euphoric. I was a still-young man, sitting a room away from his pro baseball jerseys framed in glass, basking in the wiggling of his toes.

This nighttime drill meant leaving to my wife the investigation of all bumps in the night, as I lay there like a slab, useless and half a man. Eventually my kid learned to call for only her mom when she needed something.

Most fathers think about walking their daughters down the aisle. I only dreamed of walking mine back to bed.

Since my second Deep Brain Stimulation surgery, I'd improved enough that even when I was off my medication, I was still able walk around, get food and drinks, and do the little things my daughter asked of me.

But I hadn't had the chance to do the one thing I'd always wanted to.

On this particular night I woke up and heard Makena walking down the hallway. The sound of her footsteps sent me into action, as I'd rehearsed this event a million times in my head. I got up and walked to our door, where I met her with a "Shhhh."

She had her little turtle nightlight, which was emitting tiny glowing spires that set off her sparkly Tinkerbell pajamas. Her hair was a massive confusion of yellow curls. Just looking at her for the first time in that "confused middle of the night" moment, I felt my heart lift.

"What's wrong?" I asked.

"Can't sleep," she replied. "Just can't."

I took her hand in mine, and escorted her back to her room.

I laid down with her, nose to nose. "Close your eyes," I said. "Try to go back to sleep with me."

She did this for about two minutes. Then for the next hour she tickled my face as I pretended to sleep.

I finally surrendered and made my 4:30 a.m. march downstairs, this time with her in my arms. We got some cereal, folded our bodies into my chair, watched "Tangled," and for two hours were a thicket of giggles.

Parkinson's had so stolen much from us. I don't pretend to understand the riddle of this disease. But I do know it met me where I was and didn't leave me where it found me.

There's no way I'd have understood the awesomeness of a seemingly fractional moment like this one without Parkinson's; without having my first DBS surgery fail to the extent that I almost lost my life.

I used to think that my being a champion depended on what I did when nobody else was watching. Now I know it's about what I do before the eyes of one.

A little over a year ago, through the fog of infection and a netherworld where I was more disease than man, I sent out tiny prayers to God like those streams of light from my daughter's toy, begging for one more chance to be this little girl's father.

There we sat as night became day. I smoothed her hair. I smelled her neck. I heard her laugh. I closed my eyes.

And I said, "Thank you."

***

ABOUT PARKINSON'S

Parkinson's disease is a degenerative disorder of the central nervous system. The motor symptoms of Parkinson's disease result from the death of dopamine-generating cells in the *substantia nigra*, a region of the midbrain. The cause of this cell death is unknown. Early in the course of the disease, the most obvious symptoms are movement-related; these include shaking, rigidity, slowness of movement and difficulty with walking and gait. Later, cognitive and behavioral problems may arise, with dementia commonly occurring in advanced stages of the disease. Other symptoms include sensory, sleep and emotional problems. PD is more common in the elderly. The average age of onset is around 60. Between 5-10% of cases, classified as young onset, begin between the ages of 20 and 50. PD is the second most common neurodegenerative disorder after Alzheimer's disease.

To find out more about Parkinson's disease, or you or a loved one is suffering from the disease and require support, please direct your attention to The Michael J. Fox Foundation for Parkinson's Research.

Please visit www.michaeljfox.org or call 1-800-708-7644.

If you are affected by Young-Onset Parkinson's, please also direct your attention to the Brian Grant Foundation.

Please visit www.briangrant.org, or call (503) 265-1560.

ABOUT THE AUTHORS

(Please note that a profile of Ben Petrick that originally appeared in the Jan. 9, 2012, edition of ESPN The Magazine *is reprinted with permission in the rear of this book. It is titled "Each Day I Get A Little Stronger About Being Weaker.")*

<u>BEN PETRICK</u>

Ben grew up in Hillsboro, Oregon, where he starred in three sports at Glencoe High School. During his senior football season, Ben rushed the Crimson Tide to a state championship, and was selected as Oregon's Offensive Player of the Year, while also being named All-State on defense as a safety.

After a senior baseball season in which he hit .524 with 11 HR, 45 RBI and 22 stolen bases, Ben was taken by the Colorado Rockies in the second round of the 1995 amateur draft. Ben was rated as one of the top 100 prospects in baseball from 1997-1999, and in 1999 he started at catcher in the first All-Star Futures Game at Fenway Park, playing alongside Alfonso Soriano, Mark Mulder, Lance Berkman and Pat Burrell. In September, Ben was called up to the Major Leagues, lacing an RBI double in his first at bat. He finished the season hitting .323 with 4 HR and 12 RBI in just 19 games.

Ben experienced his first symptoms of Parkinson's disease in Fall 1999, and was diagnosed with "Parkinsonism" in May 2000. Ben still managed to play four more big-league seasons for the Rockies and Detroit Tigers, while largely keeping his diagnosis a secret. Ben experienced more on-field success in 2000, hitting .322 with 3 HR and 20 RBI in 52 games; however, his performance started to slide in 2001, and he was traded to Detroit in mid-2003.

Only when he retired in 2004 did he announce publicly that he had Parkinson's disease — the same disease with which his father, Vern, had been diagnosed just seven months prior to Ben.

Ben returned to Hillsboro, marrying longtime girlfriend Kellie Starkey, and moved onto the same street where his parents and brother lived. He eventually became primary daytime caregiver to his daughter, Makena, while Kellie taught third grade.

With his Parkinson's symptoms growing worse, in December 2009 Ben elected to undergo a risky and invasive procedure known as Deep Brain Stimulation. Infection that resulted from the surgery nearly killed him. Still, Ben courageously underwent the surgery a second time a year later, this time emerging with miraculous results, as his Parkinson's symptoms were lessened to a great degree.

Today, Ben is again active in baseball, coaching at Glencoe High and providing private instruction. He is an advocate for Parkinson's research, traveling the country to speak at various events that benefit the cause. Ben is also founder of Faith In The Game (www.faithinthegame.tumblr.com), a blog containing written submissions by prominent athletes of faith. He lives in Hillsboro with his wife and two daughters.

SCOTT BROWN

Scott is from Oakland, Calif., where he attended Bishop O'Dowd High School before going on to Santa Clara University, where he played baseball. He's won several national awards for his writing and editing, and in 2001 was granted a fellowship to Duke University's DeWitt Wallace Center for Media & Democracy. His creative efforts also include a handful of film and video projects. In addition to these endeavors, Scott is a content developer and media strategist, running a collective called Imagine Media with a client roster that includes corporations in the Fortune 100, Silicon Valley tech companies, and leading media firms.

Scott has also written dog calendars, bagpiper brochures, and copy for a coffin website. He is co-creator of Faith in the Game and his two daughters.

'EACH DAY I GET A LITTLE STRONGER ABOUT BEING WEAKER'

No one will ever see it again: A 24-year old going yard off Hall of Famers while hiding Parkinson's.

But Ben Petrick didn't reach his full potential until he revealed the truth.

By Steve Wulf, *ESPN The Magazine*

(Reprinted from Jan. 9, 2012)

In the living room of a lovely home at the end of an oak tree-lined lane in Hillsboro, Ore., Ben Petrick inserts a disc into the DVD player. His wife, Kellie, has taken their 4-year-old daughter, Makena, upstairs for a nap, giving Petrick the opportunity to flop into his easy chair and fast-forward to the moment he wants you to see.

The video is of June 29, 2001, and Petrick is batting sixth as a catcher for the Colorado Rockies. With one out and nobody on in the top of the seventh as the Rockies trail the Diamondbacks 3-0, Petrick puts a perfect swing on a 2-2 fastball from Randy Johnson, launching the pitch into the leftfield seats at Bank One Ballpark for his ninth homer of the season. It's a thing of beauty.

But that's not what he wants to show you—Petrick is not one to brag, even if he did go deep off a future Hall of Famer. No, he wants to show you what happened after he hit the home run. "Watch as I run around the bases," he says. "Look at my left arm. It's not in sync with my right. It's just sort of hanging there."

He has other video evidence: a quaking left hand as he gives the target behind the plate, his difficulty removing a shin guard off his left leg after a double and a left leg spasm just before he goes the other way off CC Sabathia. Petrick played 240 major league games, with at least 221 of them coming after young-onset Parkinson's disease began to take over his 22-year-old body in 2000.

The Rockies saw so much potential that they gave Petrick a $495,000 signing bonus after drafting him from Hillsboro's Glencoe High School, near Portland. He didn't disappoint after his September 1999 call-up. Having already torn through two levels of the minors, Petrick hit four homers, drove in 12 runs and batted .323 in 19 games.

"Think Buster Posey with speed," says Pirates manager Clint Hurdle, who met Petrick as a minor league hitting instructor and later managed him in the bigs. "He had five tools, six counting his ability to handle pitchers."

"He could've been one of the best catchers ever," says Brent Butler, a Rockies infielder who roomed with Petrick. "I'm not just saying that. I truly believe it."

"He had no ceiling," says Rockies executive vice president Dan O'Dowd, the general manager who ended up trading Petrick to the Detroit Tigers in 2003 because he wasn't quite living up to his potential. "I only wish I'd known."

Who could have known? Who could have known that a player some considered a potential Hall of Fame catcher, a player who represented the traditional sense of NEXT in sports, would have his future stolen from him by an incurable disease that rarely afflicts people as young as 22?

How good was Petrick? Go back and look at his stats. In those 240 games for the Rockies and Tigers, he hit .257 with 27 home runs and 94 RBIs while trying to control the symptoms of Parkinson's, which include tremors, rigidity and slow movements. He was not only tough enough to be a catcher, the most demanding position on the field, but also athletic enough to play centerfield when he wasn't behind the plate.

"Looking back, I am amazed at what he accomplished," says Rockies first baseman Todd Helton, who was Colorado's first pick in the 1995 draft, the year Petrick was taken in the second round. "It's hard enough performing at the highest level of this game, which he did. On top of that, he had to fight off a disease that robbed him of his physical ability.

And on top of that, he had to play under the tremendous pressure of hiding the effects of that disease."

Helton pauses. "You know what, though?" he says. "I'm more impressed by what he's done with his life since."

As it turns out, Ben Petrick lost one gift and found another.

> **Looking back I was the epitome of a duck swimming in a pond. I tried to appear calm and in control, but under the water my legs were going 100 mph. — Post on Faith in the Game , April 22, 2011**
>
> Petrick comes running back from his SUV with the keys for the Glencoe locker room. In that brief sprint — and it is a full sprint — he shows no signs of Parkinson's effects. "Oh yeah, I can still run," he says with a smile.

While he still looks as athletic as in his playing days, he shakes, bobs and weaves ever so mildly as he moves down the hallway, like a top just as the spin begins to slow down. The disease causes a catch-22 in movement disorders. Without medication, people with Parkinson's become slow-moving statues for long stretches of time. With medication, they gain some mobility but experience involuntary movements, a symptom known as dyskinesia.

In the hallways, coaches chat with him about the upcoming football game and the sad state of the current program, and the teachers ask after his mom and dad. The school itself hasn't changed much since he began to fill the trophy cases that are next to the Vern Petrick Gymnasium — named for his father, Glencoe's longtime athletic director. His older brother, Rian, and younger sister, Mari Lyn, are also represented in the cases, but Petrick was the child destined for greatness.

Rian, who is the principal of nearby Evergreen Middle School, recalls a game of Hungry Hungry Hippos when he was about 11 and Ben was 6. "He started trash-talking me, so I chased him out of the house and around the neighborhood — but I couldn't catch him," Rian says. "He was faster. That's when I knew he was going to be something special."

How special? In his senior year, as a six-foot, 195-pound tailback, Petrick gained almost 2,000 total yards and scored 24 touchdowns to lead the Crimson Tide to the 1994 Class 4A State Championship. After the varsity basketball season ("not my best sport," he says), Petrick hit .524 in 25 games with 11 homers, 46 RBIs and 22 stolen bases, and he was named Oregon's 1995 baseball player of the year.

"I first saw him the summer after his junior year," says Greg Hopkins, the scout who signed him for the Rockies. "I thought I was looking at the next Dale Murphy, who's also from Portland. So I was ecstatic when the scouting director called to tell me we got him. He really was a first-round pick. Arizona State wanted him to play football, so maybe teams were afraid of that."

Continuing the tour of the school, Petrick goes back outside into the drizzle — it is Oregon, after all — and into the first base dugout of Ben Petrick Baseball Field. Looking out to Glencoe Road way beyond the leftfield fence, he says, "I hit it out into the street once. Baseball was so easy then."

In the 1995 instructional league, the Rockies had their first two picks, Helton and Petrick, room together. "I came from a football background too," says Helton, who was Peyton Manning's backup at Tennessee. "So we hit it off, even though I was coming out of college and he was coming out of high school. Man, every night: 100 sit-ups and 100 pushups. I think that's the last time I did that."

Those first few years in the minors, though, were a scuffle for Petrick.

"I remember calling my dad in tears and telling him it was too hard," he says. "Early in the '99 season, I was really struggling at Carolina, and after one night game I refused to go into the clubhouse because I was afraid I might bust it up. So I just lay on the grass, and—not to get too spiritual about it — I prayed for some assistance. Suddenly, I felt calm, and I went back in and asked the manager, Jay Loviglio, if I could keep playing. He left me in the lineup, and I hit for the cycle and went on a tear that took me to Triple-A."

That surge helped Petrick secure a spot in the first Futures Game, an event during All-Star week in which he played alongside top minor league prospects like Lance Berkman, Michael Cuddyer and Vernon Wells at Fenway Park. In

September, the Rockies called him up, and the rookie became the toast of Denver. "His future could not have been brighter," says Hurdle.

Two months later, while playing in the Arizona Fall League, Petrick tried to type an e-mail and noticed that his left hand wasn't able to keep up with his right.

> **People often say to me something to the effect of, "Wow, I'll bet your disease gives you a whole new outlook on life." I understand their reasons for saying this. But thanks to two amazing parents, perspective is not something I've lacked. — May 2, 2011**

Vern and Marci Petrick are sitting by the woodstove in the living room of their home, which is on the same street where their two sons live. Vern, 66, is retired, but woodworking, babysitting and Bible study keep him busy.

"We have so many memories," says Vern.

"Great memories of all the kids," says Marci. More than a few of them fill the den next door. With all the trophies, plaques and photos, it's practically a Petrick Hall of Fame.

"When you're a coach, you dream one of your players is going to reach the top," says Vern. "So imagine how I felt when the one player I helped to the top turned out to be my son. What a blessing."

The Petricks talk a lot about blessings, but as plentiful as those have been, they can also count a few things on the other side of the ledger. Rian's wife, Melissa, has multiple sclerosis, and Mari Lyn's infant son just had corrective surgery on one of his lungs. Then there's the specter of Parkinson's. In November 1999, just as the Rockies were penciling in Petrick as their catcher of the future, doctors diagnosed Vern with the disease.

Petrick and his friend, editor Scott Brown, maintain a website called Faith in the Game. In a tribute to his father called "The Astronaut" (Aug. 26, 2011), Petrick wrote: "He was revered at our high school. But as his health declined, kids he was in the midst of disciplining literally just ran away from him because they knew he couldn't catch up. Eventually, he had to retire from a job that fed his soul, years before he'd hoped to."

Shortly after Petrick's e-mail incident — which he shrugged off—he noticed a light tremor in his left hand when he picked up a glass. He brought it to the attention of his team's trainers, and when he went to Denver for an off-season workout, the Rockies team doctor ran a battery of tests for tumors, multiple sclerosis and other likely culprits.

They all came back negative, which was reassuring, but by the time spring training in Tucson, Ariz., rolled around, Petrick was experiencing additional symptoms and becoming increasingly frightened. In May, movement-disorder specialists in Denver gave him some hand mobility tests and told him he had a "Parkinsonism," a symptom of the disease but not necessarily the disease itself. After all, he seemed too young even for young-onset Parkinson's, which accounts for only 5% of all cases of the disease.

At first, his tremors were mild, especially compared with his father's. But the symptoms worsened month by month, confirming his darkest fears. As Petrick says, "My fate was sealed."

First identified by English physician James Parkinson in 1817, Parkinson's disease remains as insidious as ever. A progressive, neurodegenerative disorder, Parkinson's causes dopamine-producing cells to die off in the brain region that controls movement, eventually resulting in physical ramifications, such as tremors and frozen stretches.

While the disease is life-altering, it's not life-ending or even life-shortening. Medications can alleviate the symptoms, although the disease will eventually progress beyond them. Parkinson's sufferers often refer to themselves as being either "on"—the meds have kicked in, giving them some time for normal, if shake-filled, activities — or "off," at which point they become immobilized.

While it's not strictly a hereditary disease, it's likely not a total coincidence that father and son have it. Both could have been genetically susceptible to the unknown environmental trigger of the disease, be it a toxin, virus, bacteria or something else entirely.

"You can think of Parkinson's as a mystery that we try to solve," says Dr. John Nutt, who treats the Petricks and co-founded the Parkinson Center of Oregon at Oregon Health and Science University. "Or you can think of it as an adversary that we may not be able to beat but that we can outwit."

> **Vanity and insecurity filled me by the time I reached the Major Leagues. Whenever I struggled, I wondered, How must this look to others? What will others think of me when they find out I've failed? ... You can imagine, then, what being diagnosed with Parkinson's at age 22 must have done to a psyche constructed on a foundation of sand. — May 31, 2011**

Petrick is enjoying himself immensely as he scarfs down some pizza and Cold Stone ice cream while watching Game 6 of the World Series.

For one thing, he knows and played with a lot of the Cardinals and Rangers. For another, he more or less predicted the two teams would be in the Series when, on his blog in July, he asked this theological question: "What might happen if Josh Hamilton plays against Lance Berkman in the World Series this October? Both are devout, so whom does God favor?"

On this night, Berkman and the Cardinals are favored in rather unbelievable fashion, with St. Louis winning 10-9 in 11 innings. "Was that a great game or what?" Petrick asks, before succumbing to off mode.

Ten years ago, Petrick was not about to go so quietly. Parkinson's was attacking his control of the muscles and nerves that make hitting and catching 85 mph sliders possible, but he clung to his career like a baseball bat. He so desperately wanted to preserve not just his dream but also the dreams of his family and friends.

His immediate problem was that the lifestyle of baseball does not lend itself to the recommended regimen of prescription drugs. To control the Parkinson's symptoms, he began taking Requip, a drug that tricks the brain by mimicking dopamine. But long hours at the ballpark, day and night games, time zone changes and buses and planes made any sort of routine impossible. Plus, the Requip made him sleepy. "So there I was, popping pills like sunflower seeds, trying to stay awake as we go over the scouting reports of the other team, trying to pretend nothing was wrong," Petrick says. He wasn't so much deceiving his teammates as he was deceiving himself.

While most people in the Rockies organization were unaware of his situation, Petrick did confide in a select few people. Keith Dugger, the Rockies' head athletic trainer now and an assistant then, knew about Petrick's symptoms and that he took medication, but he never knew the extent of the disease or had experience dealing with it. Plus, his priority was always Petrick.

"Although we work for the team, there is a confidentiality between us and the players not unlike the doctor-patient relationship," says Dugger. His roommate Butler and a few other players also knew, but as Butler says, "When someone would notice him shaking or carrying his arm funny, Ben would totally downplay it. Besides, he was performing at a high level."

That was the thing. Even though, as Petrick points out, "there were 10 other catchers in the organization waiting to take my job," there's a place on a major league team for someone who can work and block the plate, run like a deer and hit home runs off the likes of the Big Unit.

Petrick was also immensely popular with his teammates, thanks in small part to his barbering skills. "Basically, I gave crew cuts," he says, "but I was pretty good at it." (Helton begs to differ. "There was one spring when I didn't take my hat off," he says.)

As for his meds, let's not forget the era in which he played. Quite frankly, Petrick wasn't the only Rockies player taking drugs. The difference was that the others were making themselves better than they had a right to be, while he was doing it to be normal. At one point, underwhelmed by Requip's effectiveness, he switched to another drug, Sinemet, that proved more helpful.

Even though he always passed his annual physical, Petrick's trusted few occasionally noticed a delayed reaction. "When he was catching, the high inside pitch would sometimes get by him for a passed ball because he couldn't get his glove hand up in time," says Dugger.

Petrick recalls other incidents that nearly blew his cover. In one, a sliding opponent spiked his left forearm, causing his left hand to shake so badly that he refused to remove his glove. In another, he took a pitch off his helmet. During the concussion test, "you have to put your hands out in front of you, spread your fingers and touch your nose," Petrick says. "But I couldn't spread the fingers on my left hand. I had to use my right hand to pry it open while trying to act normal."

Petrick wasn't normal though, even if he couldn't admit it, and he blamed himself for his shortcomings. In a telling 2005 story in the *Portland Tribune*, Petrick described his state of mind as a player when "things didn't click." He would ask himself, "Was it the disease or was it my skills or a combination?"

He wasn't the only one ignoring the elephant in the room. "We denied the impact: 'Hey, Ben, you're in a funk, you'll turn it around,' " Rian admitted.

In hindsight, says Nutt, "I am amazed that he was able to accomplish

as much as he did." At the time, the Rockies could see only that he wasn't the full-time catcher they thought he would be. In July 2003, still thinking Petrick's symptoms were minor, the Rockies traded him to the Tigers for right-handed pitcher Adam Bernero. The Tigers were given his medical file and asked about the tremors during his physical. But because the symptoms weren't noticeable—he had taken his meds—he passed the exam, as he always had.

His stay in Detroit lasted only 43 games, though he did hit four homers and make two sensational outfield plays — throwing out Frank Thomas of the White Sox at the plate

167

from center and going over the wall in left at Detroit's Comerica Park to rob Twins infielder Chris Gomez of a home run. However, Petrick felt increasingly guilty about deceiving people, particularly his teammates—"that maybe by me playing I was making our team worse," he says.

By the following spring, with his dyskinesia worsening, Petrick was released from a minor league contract after he went 0-for-10 to start the season with the Tigers' Triple-A affiliate, the Toledo Mud Hens. As he drove back to Oregon, he made up his mind to quit — until he got an offer from the Padres' Triple-A affiliate in Portland. Though he managed to hit two more homers, the struggle had become too much. In May 2004, Petrick announced his retirement and openly revealed that he was suffering from young-onset Parkinson's.

While that was that for baseball, the rest of his life beckoned. And that life involved Kellie Starkey. The two attended the same high school but were four years apart. They didn't meet until her senior year; the following fall, the Rockies called him up. "So here I am," he says, "a major league rookie in love with a beautiful hometown girl, when all of a sudden, my body starts telling me something I don't want to hear."

"I remember Ben saying he didn't think he could ask Kellie to marry him with Parkinson's and all," Marci Petrick says. "And I said, 'Why don't you let her make that decision?' "

So shortly after she received her master's degree from the University of Oregon and he retired from playing, Kellie and

Ben married in Hawaii and honeymooned on a cruise to Alaska. "I knew what I was getting into," says Kellie, who is a third-grade teacher at her old elementary school. "Well, maybe not everything."

> **I would not dignify Parkinson's with my emotions. It had stolen my career, my money, my body, my father's body, my parents' golden years, and a large measure of joy in daily life from my entire family. But it would not take my toughness.**
> **— April 22, 2011**

When Petrick totters into a burger restaurant and slides into the booth, the sideways glance of the waitress seems to say, "Do I need to cut this guy off?" He takes the waitress off the hook by ordering a soda as he, Kellie and Makena decide what to order for dinner. Petrick notices these things, but they no longer bother him.

"I remember a conversation I had with Michael J. Fox," he says. "I asked him if he minded the stares in public, and he said—pardon my language — 'F— vanity.' "

In the years right after his retirement, Petrick helped with the Glencoe football and baseball teams and became active in Parkinson's causes. "I could still nearly hide my symptoms from people when I was off," he says. But the dyskinesia got worse in part, he says, because he had taken so much medication in hopes of prolonging his career. He became as frustrated with the disease as he had with baseball in those early years in the minors.

There he was, the Golden Boy of Hillsboro, afraid to go out in public, in need of help to tie his shoelaces.

As he's written, "I was suddenly, acutely aware of the fact that I'd left town as an object of everyone's envy and returned the object of everyone's pity." Or, as Kellie says, "He had gone from being defined by baseball to being defined by Parkinson's."

The disease is so frustrating and baffling that unlikely causation theories abound. One idea that gets floated is that the *Borealis burgdorferi* bacteria that causes Lyme disease also causes Parkinson's.

For a while, Petrick pursued some alternative treatments in that area.

"We have had some disagreements," says Julie Carter, another of his doctors at OHSU, "but we also feel that it's important that our patients feel in control of their treatment."

Another theory is that Parkinson's is somehow stress-related — "Ben did put a lot of pressure on himself," says his mother — and it is true that stress can temporarily exacerbate the symptoms. Nutt maintains that the theory with the most evidence is that Parkinson's is somehow related to pesticides and herbicides. As far as Petrick is concerned, "My interest in the cause has less to do with my case than it does in helping to find the cure."

After Makena was born in 2007, Kellie encouraged Ben to pursue deep brain stimulation to improve his off time and increase his on time. Another top-level athlete with young-onset Parkinson's, cyclist Davis Phinney, the first American to win a stage of the Tour de France, had undergone DBS and recommended the procedure to Petrick.

In DBS, a surgeon implants an electrode into the part of the brain where the nerve signals are generating the Parkinson's symptoms; the patient is kept awake to provide feedback to make sure that the precise brain target has been stimulated. Two years ago, Petrick underwent DBS at the Stanford Medical Center, and the procedure went startlingly well. "I was on, but without medicine," he remembers. However, while recovering at home, Petrick went into a series of seizures and had to be rushed to OHSU, where doctors discovered an infection in his brain and had to remove the electrode. He spent the next several nights surrounded by family and friends.

Rian still chokes up over that time. "Such an awful period," he says. "My little brother, who was our big hero … we didn't know if he was going to make it."

Erik Aartsen, Petrick's best friend, who is a system engineer, grew up on "Petrick Lane" and felt like part of the family, so he offered to take one of the night shifts. "He was in such pain that he was in tears, sobbing, standing on the bed," Aartsen says. "And this was not a guy who ever gave up. Ever. Then he grabbed my hand, and he asked me to pray with him.

"Suddenly, he calmed down. I felt a sense of relief come over me too."

Each day, I get a little stronger about being weaker. — Sept . 19, 2011

Makena has to get dressed before she goes off to a rehearsal for a school production of *The Wizard of Oz* — typecast, she plays a Munchkin. Before she leaves, she climbs on Petrick's broad shoulders, and they laugh together as she hangs around his neck and tries to tickle him.

It's a thing of beauty.

So is this, a passage from "Night Becomes Us," which Petrick posted a few months after undergoing his second DBS procedure a year ago at OHSU:

> **My 3-year-old daughter's voice woke me up at 2:30 last night. It was a moment I'd been waiting for since the day she was born.**
>
> **At night I don't take any medication for my Parkinson's disease, ceding to my wife all nighttime duties, as I lay there, useless and feeling like not much of a man.**
>
> **Most fathers think about walking their daughters down the aisle. I only dreamed of walking mine back to bed. ...**
>
> **Since my DBS surgery, I have improved enough so that off medication I am still able to walk**

around, get food and drinks, and do the little things my daughter might ask of me. But I hadn't had the chance to do the one thing I'd always wanted to ...

Last night, I woke up and heard my daughter walking down the hallway. The sound of those footsteps sent me into action. I got up and walked to our door, where I met her with a "Shhhh." She had her little turtle night-light, which was emitting tiny glowing spires that set off her sparkly Tinker Bell pajamas. Her hair was a massive confusion of yellow curls.

Just looking at her for the first time in that "confused middle of the night" moment, I felt my heart lift.

"What's wrong?" I asked.

"Can't sleep," she replied. "Just can't."

I stuck my hand out and enveloped hers, and escorted her back to her room.

I lied down with her, nose to nose. "Close your eyes," I said. "Try to go back to sleep with me."

She followed my example for about two minutes. Then for the next hour she tickled my face as I pretended to sleep.

I ultimately surrendered and made my 4:30 a.m. march downstairs, this time with her in my arms. We got some cereal, folded our bodies into my chair, watched Tangled, and for two hours were a thicket of giggles.

There were many times that I resented the perspective Parkinson's gave me. But now I thank God for it. There is no way I'd understand the awesomeness of a seemingly fractional moment like this without this disease; without having my first DBS surgery fail to the extent that I almost lost it all. This is why I feel that God is at work in my life ...

There we sat in our glowing house as night became day. I smoothed her hair. I smelled her neck. I heard her laugh. I closed my eyes.

And I said, "Thank you."

Funny how life echoes. A horrible night at the plate in Double-A followed by a renewed sense of purpose. A horrible night in the hospital followed by the epiphany that there was still so much to live for. Despite the disastrous consequences of the first DBS, Petrick decided it was worth the risk to try again. While he still takes medication, the quality of his off time has improved immensely.

"Prior to surgery, it would literally take me five minutes — and it was a labored five minutes — to go from our bedroom to the chair downstairs," he says. That's no longer the case, with his mobility increasing threefold when he's off and his dyskinesia becoming much less severe; the only downside is a tendency to slur his words.

So what's next for Petrick?

Outlined against a blue-gray October sky, two men climb through the stands, up onto the roof and into the press box of Hare Field, Glencoe's football stadium. Petrick and Aartsen, an old teammate, are there to tape the school's game with visiting Forest Grove. They could be home watching Game 7 of the World Series instead of filming a battle in the drizzle between a pair of 2–6 teams, but this is what they do every week to help restore their alma mater to its football glory. "Not exactly *Friday Night Lights*," says Petrick.

The important thing is that he's out and about again. Last March, the Petricks traveled to Arizona for spring training to catch up with some of the teammates he had been avoiding for years. "Seeing how well he's doing, watching the three of them together was … well, it was pretty cool," says Helton.

He's a full-time dad of a young girl who knows a great deal about Parkinson's. "She'll sometimes tell people, 'Daddy's off now,' " Petrick says, with some pride.

And he's also a full-time son. "In a weird way, it's kind of nice that my dad and I both have Parkinson's," says Petrick.

"We understand what we're going through, what the on and off cycles are like. You should've seen us this summer. We built a redwood deck together, and if anybody walked by and saw us shaking and walking around like we were drunk, they wouldn't have known what to make of it."

Father and son have something else in common—a positive attitude in the face of a disease that would entitle them to feel sorry for themselves. "I might have Parkinson's," as Vern likes to say, "but Parkinson's doesn't have me."

"We light up every time the Petricks come into the office," says Nutt.

With better treatments and the increased pace of research, maybe Petrick can stay one step ahead of this degenerative disease. He always was fast.

Then there's Faith in the Game, which he started last April, and an e-book. Both have led to numerous speaking engagements, helping him find a voice he never knew he had.

Oh, and one more thing:

Kellie is due in January.

(The following is reprinted with permission from the January 9, 2012, edition of ESPN The Magazine.)